Enough Is Enough

ENOUGH IS ENOUGH

Exploding the Myth of
——————*Having It All*——————

Carol Orsborn

G. P. PUTNAM'S SONS NEW YORK

G. P. Putnam's Sons
Publishers Since 1838
200 Madison Avenue
New York, NY 10016

Typeset by Fisher Composition, Inc.

Library of Congress Cataloging-in-Publication Data

Orsborn, Carol.
Enough is enough.

1. Women—United States—Life skills guides.
2. Women—United States—Time management.
3. Work and family—United States.   I. Title.
HQ1221.O66   1986   640'.43'088042   86-12201
ISBN 0-399-13175-2

Printed in the United States of America
1   2   3   4   5   6   7   8   9   10

This handbook is for . . .

Betty, Bobbie, Mae, Christine, Sara, Mary, Cathy, Carol, Suzy and all of us who have refused to give up our dreams, even though the harder we tried to reach them, the further they seemed to slip away.

This is for all the times we thought we found the answer to happiness, only to discover that the complications outweighed the benefits. This is for the children we chose to have head-on with careers and involvements; and for the children we didn't have.

This is for the life-style we worked so hard to achieve—as our conversation faded from hopes for the future into mortgage payments. This is for the fear that if we were to take time off from work or try to change our careers in hopes of finding something more satisfying, our family finances would be thrown into havoc.

This is for all the times we stood each other up for lunch—and truly understood. This is for all the diets we've started and failed, for the aerobics class that turned out to be too tough. This is for feeling guilty when we sat down in the middle of the day to read a book. This is for trying to be everything we could be and feeling inadequate still. This is for our courage, as we began to tell each other the truth. This is for your love and support, as you encouraged me to make our private conversations public.

This is for sharing the belief that it wasn't just that I had a particularly miserable group of friends—that, just maybe, the feelings we shared while walking the kids to school, during coffee breaks in the office, in brief snatches of phone calls early in the morning or late at night—belonged to our entire generation of women.

And most of all, this handbook is for my family—Dan, Grant and Jody—who let themselves be bullied, cajoled and occasionally inspired into traveling a road that could lead to something higher than coping on the scale of human experience. For believing that there could be joy and fun, intimacy and love beyond anything we had yet experienced in our fast-track lives.

This handbook is for life, given to all of us who truly deserve to be happy—and who are blessed with everything we need to achieve that.

This handbook is for anyone who understands that there is honor in telling the truth about what isn't working and what is— honor in being a beginner.

This handbook is one place to begin.

Special thanks for support of my organization and book to Dr. Lloyd Matzkin, Mae Matzkin, Cathy Holmes, Christine Kerr, Sybil Boutilier, Tim Dewar and the staff of The Orsborn Group Public Relations: Bill, Elizabeth, Ellen and Valerie.

I dedicate this book to you, my brother Gene.

OFFICIAL HANDBOOK OF
SUPERWOMEN'S ANONYMOUS

CONTENTS

MY NAME IS CAROL ORSBORN.
I AM A RECOVERING SUPERWOMAN.
THIS IS MY STORY.

Superwomen's Anonymous
Handbook Pledge

Raise your right hand and repeat after me:

I pledge to read only as much of this as I want, when I want, even if it means stopping in the middle of a sentence.

THANKSGIVING DAY, CIRCA MID-1980s

When an article on you and the international self-help group for women you've founded has just appeared in the A section of *The New York Times,* you wouldn't expect to find yourself—within a mere handful of days—sitting at the Thanksgiving table feeling small enough to crawl inside the turkey, stuffing and all. You wouldn't expect to, but there I was: surrounded by successful friends and family, and our much-loved children of assorted ages, accomplishments and school tuitions, not only feeling small enough to crawl inside, but wanting to.

Thanksgiving brings out the superwoman in the best of us. It wasn't enough that the organization I had founded, Superwomen's Anonymous, had scored a big hit nationally. Not enough that I had earned my brown belt, and successfully ran a nationally recognized independent public relations agency; that I'd even managed to deliver my husband and children to my parents' house for this special holiday—and not one of them had a cold.

There I was, watching my mother heave the thirty-pound bird on the table, dishing up more species of potatoes than I knew existed. Growing up next to this dynamo was a never-ending race to a mythological finish line. My earliest memories are of my chubby little legs chugging as fast as they could go as mom navigated the aisles of Marshall Field's department store with a messianic zeal. The mission: a pink bow for my hair, black patent leather shoes and a Shirley Temple dress. Exactly the kind my one-year-old was now smearing sweet potato on.

My cousin Janet's daughter is one, and you don't see her smearing sweet potato all over her pretty dress—now do you? This was the first of many thoughts that sent me deep into the stuffing. Not only does Janet's daughter not smear, but she can point—on command—to pictures not only of cats, not only of dogs, but of various species of rare butterflies. I love Janet, despite the fact that she has declared—at this very table—that, unlike me, she would never have a child while trying to continue her career. She quit work when she was pregnant. Good for her word, she did not continue her career. She changed careers. She now runs an architectural firm.

I suppose I was feeling particularly vulnerable on this occasion in the shadow of my mother's awesome culinary accomplishments. In the recent past, I'd had wonderful conversations with each of my table companions, in keeping with the philosophy I'd been discovering over the past year. It had been a year of incredible joy but also of pain as I reached out from my private reservoir of fear of personal inadequacy—fear that, while I looked to all the world like a woman who had it all, I still had the audacity to feel unfulfilled.

Through a series of miracles, I woke up from my lonely

vigil—only to discover that my ever-expanding circle of friends were in the same boat.

Together, we began pulling the oars through the crises of our lives—big and small. The first step had been admitting to each other how we really felt.

• Janine, whose son was to be held back in first grade because he failed to learn to read. The school psychologist's appraisal: suppressed anxiety.

• Julia, so ashamed of the fact that she did not work for money that she single-handedly ran an alphabet soup of community organizations. She was too busy to read any of the books she so eagerly checked out of the library every week.

• Suzan, whose triumphant career path led her to world travel—and away from what had once been a happy marriage.

That first step was an important one: it wasn't just me; I wasn't alone.

Each of us now sitting at that Thanksgiving table, and every one of the more than 2000 women who had written to join my organization, had their story. I was bolstered by the knowledge that the new way I was thinking about my life had helped bring ease to so many closet tensions, and not just for my friends and members, but also for my family and myself.

As I looked around the table, I realized that in some ways nothing had changed over the past year. Julia was still bragging about her daughter's private school curriculum—including her child's creation of a computer game based on Shakespeare's sonnets. My son's table decoration, the result of *his* curriculum—a potato-shaped turkey, crayons stuck in for legs—stared at me.

Were we falling behind? Permanently lapsed? Then another miracle occurred. Something that let me know that things had changed, and changed quite a lot since previous Thanksgivings. I remembered to laugh.

PART I

Why Me?

_____*Chapter One*_____

EVERYTHING SHE CAN BE . . .

MAY, 1985

"What advice do you have for women who want to experience the kind of success you have?"

The young business reporter had to wait so long for my response that moss started to grow on her eager smile. I looked at her—she was so earnest, so admiring. Do I tell her the truth? I wrestled with the thought. It would have been so much safer to run through the litany of role-model slogans: commitment, hard work, coping, balancing, juggling. I had built a business and a life on these virtues. While I was undergoing a transformation internally, did I dare share the quiet rebellion that was going on inside me with my community, my peers and my business associates?

Here was my conference room—a table large enough to sit twelve. Once there used to be staff meetings so large, some of the more enterprising senior executives took to selling table space to the interns. On the wall were clippings from newspapers and magazines from around the country—mostly placements we had made for our clients, a veritable Who's Who of law firms, consumer products and hotels. Mixed in was a history of clippings about some businesswoman who managed to balance family and career while going after her brown belt in karate and writing several unpublished novels. So much had changed for me since those articles had been written, I barely remembered that the businesswoman was me.

Once—and not that long ago—I had assumed that the disassociation I felt from my own success came from some personal inadequacy, some gene for happiness that had been missing at birth. I was the woman who had everything—and I felt empty inside. I kept waiting for something wonderful to click on permanently. But success seemed, at best, a minor buzz that lasted not more than five minutes after the gift was unwrapped, the house bought, the deal consummated, the article published.

My kind of success? It had been much too recently that I'd been in my doctor's office talking through the Kleenex about the stresses and strains of my complicated life. In the depths of what textbooks call postpartum depression, I knew darn well that hormones did not create the steep mortgage we had to struggle to meet. Newborn babies who cried everytime a client was on the phone. An older son with sudden allergies to dust. I watched my life fall apart, as my husband continued on with the karate classes we'd been taking together—leaving me behind as he moved through degrees of brown belt that were rightfully mine. We were, textbook-proofed, the ideal family of the eighties, down to the dream home—bay view, household help, meaningful hobbies, and two-point-zero children—a boy and now a baby girl.

The doctor's voice was soothing, calming—"Your plate is too full," he said. "Learn to relax. Take some time for yourself. It's simply not worth it."

Not worth it? I looked up at him, ready to ask him what I could possibly give up, when I realized that he had left the room.

Great advice, I thought—running to pick up my younger from daycare, my elder from soccer, and our dinner from the gourmet take-out.

"Too bad it doesn't apply to me." Hopelessly optimistic, I was certain that there was something more I could do that would lead me to happiness.

I left the doctor's office determined to do something about my life.

I bought a microwave oven.

Microwave ovens cook frozen dinners quite nicely—but they do not lead to happiness. Neither does reading about how to cook a bake-ahead casserole, get your kid into the right kindergarten, and cope, balance and juggle what always turned out to be one piece too many.

I was sick of hearing celebrity after celebrity admit that they "once had problems coping, but have finally learned to balance their priorities." Just once, I screamed at the talk show host on our living room set—let me hear someone—anyone—say, "Yeah, it's tough. I'm a mess."

Just once, show me a commercial with a woman frying up the bacon, taking care of the kids, getting gussied up for a night on the town . . . and too damned tired to press the button on the hairspray can.

I had spent thirty-five years trying to have, do and be everything I could. I had been a good mother, good boss, good wife, good daughter, good role model—and now I knew I was good and miserable. I also knew, however, how to put up a good fight. Rather than sink quietly into misery, I threw myself into a search for solutions. Having exhausted our country's mass-marketed philosophies, I turned to other cultures. I continued my exploration of Eastern thought. When I entered libraries and book stores, certain books mysteriously found their way into my hands. I devoured

Scott Peck's *The Road Less Traveled*, Stewart Emery's *The Owner's Manual for Your Life* and *Actualizations, Prospering Woman* by Dr. Ruth Ross. I took a creative journaling class with Sara Deutsch at the College of Marin, and "explored the riches within that had sunk to the bottom."

What I dug up was a vision of women today, standing on the balancing beam of our lives, juggling the bowling balls of family, career and personal satisfaction. We had accepted that this was the way things had to be. Our only choice was that we could do it well—or we could do it poorly. Most women's how-to books are about doing it well—and when a sixteen-pound ball is barrelling toward your head, it's nice to have some advice. In fact, you'd better be paying attention to learning the skills.

But most women's books and literature miss the point completely. Why were we picturing ourselves this way? In a moment of inspiration, I looked up "cope" in the dictionary. This is the highest experience held out as a goal for women in the eighties to achieve, and do you know what it means? To hold your own in a struggle! This is the best we can hope for, to hold our own in a struggle? Cope, balance and juggle—the three Rs of superwomanism. Instead of coping, I began to formulate a new vision of what was possible. Rather than picture ourselves struggling against the instability of a balancing beam like acrobats juggling the balls of our lives, I tried out another thought. What if I was the ball? A beautiful, multicolored ball—my choice from any within the spectrum of possibilities. Now—roll. See what happens? Each color was a different facet of myself—the things I cared about, the things I wanted to do and the things I had to do. And as the ball rolled, the different colors blended into a single one. Becoming this new color involved both pain and happiness, but somehow, as I started rolling, my feelings about myself made a subtle but miraculous shift.

As the reporter waited to hear what advice I had for

women eager for my kind of success, I heard from down the hall my husband Dan wooing some new business we would probably get. I could just see the corner of a full-color portrait of my children on my desk. Nothing looked any different from the outside, but inside, I was unleashed. It was painful and raw sometimes, ecstatic and vital others. There was some quality to what was going on inside of me that had shaken itself awake with great reluctance . . . some quality that, I now know, held the promise to me of personal change, the discovery that something might turn out for me after all.

"My advice to women?" I finally answered. Then taking a deep breath . . . did I dare? Would this be the end for me? My business down the tubes? My family ostracized? I answered honestly . . .

"Enough is enough."

"Enough?"

"Enough coping, balancing and juggling. Enough trying to have it all, enough exhaustion and personal inadequacy— enough!"

The reporter's jaw dropped as I ran down to the business Porsche to tear the bumper sticker I had placed on the front, BORN TO MAKE MONEY. "Not me!" I shouted.

I was born to be in ecstasy. Somewhere along the way, I'd begun to disengage from a track that was leading me someplace I didn't want to go. Parts of me had realized that and were busy making changes, parts of me continued on a daily routine as if under the influence of a kind of mass hypnotism. Rebellion. It felt fantastic to go public, raising my flag to let my colors fly.

I no longer accepted that my unhappiness came from some inadequacy on my part. There was something wrong with the system—with the way things had been put together. It was time to say enough is enough to all the demands and trappings that accompanied the concept of success for women in the 1980s. What would take its place, I wasn't completely sure—but, I realized, I had nothing to lose. The reporter, surprised though she was, ended up putting my picture on the front cover of the publication. I had declared myself. I had taken one small step for woman-kind.

"Maybe we can't have everything," I offered, "But maybe we don't want everything. Instead, let's have what we want."

"Enough is enough" is a motto that has since been heard around the world. At first whispered from woman to woman, at PTA meetings, in the boardrooms of corporate America, in factories deep in the South. Superwomen's Anonymous, a self-help group designed for the woman of the eighties, continued to boom on the founding platform guaranteeing no classes, no meetings, no fund-raisers. The perfect self-help group for women already overburdened and overcommitted.

The New York Times, the *Today* show, *People* magazine, *Good Morning America,* and Reuters counted the letters that were pouring in—two thousand in just a few months, from lawyers and mill workers, homemakers and politicians, with husbands and children and without. The theme was the same: if we didn't "have it all," we felt guilty; if we did, we felt exhausted. The thought was occurring to women throughout the world that if the role model of success in the 1980s was impossible to achieve, it was then possible to entertain the notion that each of us just might be free to create our own lives. As women heard the message, one by one, they actually began making changes in their lives. Having run out of external options, they began to explore internal ones. Timidly, we stuck our toes in the waters of personal and social change.

Marcia Adams, a lawyer in Palo Alto, did nothing for five minutes for the first time since her first child had been born—four years ago—and only because it was the middle of the night. A secretary in New York marched into her boss' office and courageously asked to cut back to a forty-hour week. In Duluth, a homemaker neglected to write personal messages on her Christmas cards as she had for the past five years. But this time, for the first time, her indulgence did not make her feel guilty.

There were bigger changes as well. Changes that will undoubtedly impact society as a whole. But I leave these for you to discover as this handbook unfolds.

What I did, no less than dramatically shift the course of my family's lives, is interwoven throughout the book. At this point, suffice it to say that I am a recovering superwoman. Going on two years now—and many, many moments of happiness that I once thought beyond the realm of possibility for a successful role model like me.

This handbook is written for all of us who are eager to explore an expanded world of options and opportunities. This handbook is meant to inspire you on your journey, as I have been inspired on mine.

How Far Gone Are You?

You already know you are a superwoman: or at least, that you would need to be, to accomplish all the tasks you feel you ought to undertake. You know you need something and you need it fast . . . but what, how much, how fast? Take this examination. The results will enable you to most effectively apply the principles in this handbook to your life.

Multiple Choice

The role your career plays in your life is:
  a. Satisfaction.
  b. Money.
  c. What life?

To keep your house together, you:
  a. Have occasional outside help.
  b. Have regular outside help.
  c. Clean the house yourself just before the outside
     help arrives so she won't know how messy you are.

For physical exercise you:
  a. Go to aerobics class several times a week.
  b. Run an aerobics class several times a week.
  c. Earned a seeded position for the Iron Man.

Your child has:
  a. Dark circles under the eyes.
  b. Very dark circles under the eyes.
  c. Dark circles—what eyes?

If you could only . . .
  a. Lose ten pounds . . .
  b. Let your polish dry before leaving the manicurist
     and smudging your thumbnail on the ignition . . .
  c. Sit down . . .

Your significant relationship . . .
  a. Is proud of your accomplishments.
  b. Is resentful of your schedule.
  c. Is pretty sure he would recognize you if he saw you
     on the street.

Community involvements:
  a. You volunteered to call other women to bake cakes
     for the fund-raiser.

b. You baked a cake for the fund-raising committee.
c. You *are* the fund-raising committee.

"Nurturing yourself" means to you:
  a. A big bag of Fritos.
  b. Something that happened once when you were a baby.
  c. Not applicable.

About being a superwoman:
  a. You feel proud.
  b. You feel resentful.
  c. You stopped feeling in 1966.

Analysis

If you gave yourself mostly As:

Prepeaking Superwomanitis

You are probably feeling that any day now, things will turn out for you. Of course, there are the lingering doubts and incompletions, but basically, you have hope that the next promotion will solve all your problems. Watch out. You are about to burn out.

If you gave yourself mostly Bs:

Superwoman Role-Modelitis

You've done it—reached the ideal for women in the 1980s. My condolences. So—time to stop feeling sorry for yourself. There's a big, wonderful world of exciting options out there to explore. It's up to you—and you can do it. Trust me.

If you gave yourself mostly Cs:

A Goner

Read this paragraph and then close this book. I would like you to go to the phone—quietly. Call a good friend. Preferably one with a place in the country that you can visit. When you are there and can—unprompted—hear at least two birds singing, you may continue with this book. But not until then.

_____*Chapter Two*_____

AN HISTORICAL PERSPECTIVE

I know that you think the seemingly hopeless situation
you're in is the result of a complex set of personal decisions
you've made over the years. You are absolutely willing to be
responsible for every choice, every result. In fact, if you are
like most superwomen, you are also willing to be responsible
for everything your husband, your children, and the United
States of America have done for the past several decades.

Unfortunately, most superwomen equate responsibility
with burden, and burden is more often than not guilt. Yes,
you *are* accountable for the fact that you have not created
the experience of joy and vitality you'd always imagined. But
are you guilty of it? Was some perverse gene, motivated by
unconscious desire, bound to make sure you'd be miserable
this time around?

Do you know what responsibility means? The ability to

respond. That's it. The ability to respond to external events at hand. You are present on this planet today because for millennia, the forecells of your cells proved they had the ability to respond. Each age, century and decade has had its own set of demands. During the ice age, a thick fur coat was not a luxury item. You think you are guilty of unhappiness because of a misuse of free choice. And, until recently, you probably thought you were the only one on this planet who had all the advantages, and still managed to blow it.

I'm here to tell you that you only *think* you've had free choice. In fact, our entire generation of women was molded by a complex interplay of biological, sociological and psychological factors. So was our parents' generation . . . and their parents' before that. This handbook is about to march you onto very new turf. In fact, it could be thought of as the next step of evolution for women . . . not to mention humanity. You can be among the first generation in recorded history to wake up en masse from its unconscious programming. We are at a moment of true choice for ourselves. For the first time, we are at the critical mass level of awareness that may allow us to use our keenly honed response systems—not to respond to external imperatives, but from internal ones.

History of a Superwoman
_____ *Dating from Prehistoric Times* _____

The Dawn of Life

We're talking single-celled creatures here.

Life-forms who reproduced without the commonly accepted advantages of sexual differentiation. Take the amoeba. An amoeba is an organism trying to do, have and be everything it can. It does not feel that it has any choice in the matter. The prehistoric amoeba, in addition to not having to worry about qualifying for an American Express Gold Card, did not even have the option of enrolling its offspring in soccer league.

Aside from these lost advantages, nothing much has really changed over the millennia. Consult this chart.

	SUPERWOMAN	AMOEBA
Efficient and productive	X	X
Is unable to halt body movement: always on the run/ooze.	X	X
Acts from a biological imperative to improve the species.	X	X
Feels no moral compunction about breaking lunch dates.	X	X

As single-celled creatures evolved, male and female energy began to differentiate. The following is the criterion used to determine which plasma was male, and which female:

Criterion

If you were to serve the family a piece of steak, and part of it was burned, who would get that piece?

The one who answered "Probably me" became female energy.

_____ *The Thirties and Forties* _____

Multicellular organisms, winning the battle of natural selection for a million years or two, eventually became quite adept at survival. That's lucky, because about the time they made it to my parents' generation there was a depression going on, followed by a war.

These were tough years, during which the ability to cope was an appropriate virtue. Even now, individuals who went through the Great Depression and World War II greet each other with the salutation, "How are you getting along?" They used every bit of their ability to "get by," "make do" and "handle it." And had I been in their boots, I would have done the same. There was no choice but to do what it took to survive. Dads spoon-fed their children stories of digging ditches for $16.50 a week to put themselves through school. Moms prayed for the day they could afford carpeting. Through separation of war and hardship, they held on to their abiding belief that their suffering would find meaning in the creation of a better world for their children: a place where future generations could have all the advantages.

The Fifties

Every generation in history has been born with the expectation that they will do better than their parents. For the majority of my parents' generation—born of the industrial revolution, many the children of immigrants, coming of age in a time when the prevailing ethic was merely to survive— this did not prove to be an impossible task. In fact, coming from the rear, they rode an economic boom to peaks of material and personal comfort unprecedented in human history. What a triumph, to have "pulled themselves up by their bootstraps" to give us—their children—every advantage. If they, coming from where they did—with no help or resources from anybody—could achieve what they did, just think what our generation, with all the resources in the world, should be able to accomplish? And so, a new generation of children rolled through the suburban fifties, gathering lessons, Mickey Mouse ears and every advantage denied to their parents during the hard-knock decades of their youth. Now it was up to us to make something of ourselves. After all, we had college educations, a solid financial base, and Girl Scout badges that ran up one side of the sash and down the other.

Our mothers, well schooled in the principles of self-sacrifice, gave their all for us. With hope and love for the future, they denied their own need for self-nurturing and expression. They channeled everything they had into us. With all that help behind the scenes, we were able to concentrate on the finer details: little white gloves, dancing class and piano lessons. We were being groomed to be the ultimate expression of womanhood—to be, have and do all the things previously denied to females. Watching our mothers, who gave their all and then, spent, watched their all go off to college, we determined to do things differently.

The Sixties

We would live for ourselves, for here and for now. Forget about the future—we, more than anyone, knew there was no future in it. Together, we let the fresh air of freedom in: flower power and love-ins. The sixties were a time for personal exploration, nonproductive fun that captured our attention although—or even because—they held no promise of ribbons or badges. The fresh air of freedom proved intoxicating, as women in unprecedented numbers flexed their muscles. Raised to have it all, we deserved to participate in the mainstream. We were ripe for women's liberation. We turned offending undergarments of the female gender into torches, scaring the heck out of the economic hierarchy, threatened by women's desire to participate in male-dominated careers. Women, however, schooled in the principles of survival, fought for and won the right to an expanded role in society. Many of the women on the front lines were baby boomers—too young at the time to worry about procreation and child rearing. This was liberation, and we loved every bit of it.

The Seventies

Unburdened by thoughts of children, we wed work and playmates—if we wed at all. Through our twenties and thirties, when past generations would have supported families of four, five or more on one paycheck, we explored the freedom of two paychecks per couple. Impacting the economic structure of middle class America, we traveled to Europe, brought kiwi fruit into our homes and popped for the top-of-the-line toilet paper.

At the time, it appeared that we were following in the footsteps of previous generations, though getting there more swiftly, moving into our own homes and condos at the same age that our parents had still been living with their parents. In truth, our wealth was an illusion of easy credit, coupled with dual check buying power. As members of the largest, most educated work force in history—the baby boom generation—eventually our salaries, for many of us way too soon, hit a competitive ceiling. No matter—this couldn't be happening to us. Plastic bank cards, seconds on houses and lines of credit bridged the gap as we simultaneously created and got hooked on a level of consumerism unprecedented in history. If our real wealth could not exceed that of our parents, at least our life-styles could.

The men of our generation, in the name of support for women's liberation, soon discovered a new wrinkle: that women could find satisfaction both in and out of the home— and make a few bucks to boot. So what if there wasn't a warm dinner waiting at home—there was always some chic new spot to try out, some café or *ristorante*. Not that it was all ideal. When a few bucks turned into a few bigger bucks, egos collided and skidded into divorce. But for many, there was the expression of female equality incubating. Then we hit thirty.

The Eighties

With the biological time clock chiming midnight at the exact moment our careers were peaking, we had our first clash with Mother Nature. Schooled in the knowledge that we could have, do and be everything we wanted, we marched into motherhood waving the new improved Pampers' flag of invulnerability in the face of all obstacles. We would somehow make it work. And why not—we had, after all, all the advantages.

But something beside equality was incubating. Babies. Husbands and wives who started out as kids side by side, went into deep shock as the status quo discovered some fundamental differences between mommies and daddies. With their careers at peak and their children's diapers full, a new generation of moms attempted to accomplish before nine and after five all the things moms used to do for their kids each and every day.

The media went into high gear, editorial pages pitching the concepts we were raised on from birth: managing, coping, balancing and juggling. Much like the nightmarish carnival in *Pinocchio* that we were taking our children to see at the Saturday matinee, the contemporary land of plenty was spawning its own donkey ears and tails. Tucked neatly under Lady Di hats, our ears were hearing husbands, children, supermarket clerks and cosmetic salesmen telling us that we couldn't afford not to work anymore.

Not that women didn't want to work. Of course many wanted to work. Work is fun, satisfying, fulfilling and profitable.

Maybe the problem was having children. But as you get on toward thirty or thirty-five, Mother Nature starts whispering in your ear. Could having kids possibly be a sublime experience? Guess what . . . at times, and for most of us, overall it is.

Was it the men in our life? Not doing their share? They were as confused as we were, wanting us to have what we want, but not fully understanding why they should come home from a hard day's work and be expected to be the first generation of men in American history to change a diaper.

They wanted for us what we wanted . . . but what did we want?

All of us who comb the magazines and newspapers hoping to discover the secret to a successful, happy life: career, good marriage, children, wealth, hobbies, health . . . And you know what the secret is?

We all either are already doing, or feel we ought to be doing, at least one piece too much.

One piece too much already and everyday, the media has more ideas for us. It wasn't enough that we were already doing five minutes of Air Force exercises. Along comes Jane Fonda and her sixty-minute workouts. Now that's not enough. We should be jogging. Actually, jogging was last month's prescription. Now we should be pumping iron.

How to get that promotion, how to teach your infant to read, grow your own tomatoes, bake the moistest cake for the church fund-raiser . . .

Periodically, we feel overwhelmed. When we are in pain—dramatically and publicly—then we have permission to take a break. For some, this means drugs or alcohol. For others, psychiatric care.

In my thinking, coping is the prevailing ethic of our society—keeping the lid screwed on just tight enough. We are used to stress, strain and struggle in our society. There's a certain comfort and security about it—something we share with the generations of the past. A tradition. Hopefully, one that we will not leave behind as a legacy to our children.

Chapter Three

THE SELLING OF SUPERWOMAN

A superwoman will do, have or buy virtually anything if she believes it will help her reduce the stress, strain and struggle in her life. And there are plenty of advertisers, television talk show hosts and women's magazines that are more than happy to volunteer suggestions.

Wear their perfume, and the commercial holds the promise of vitality and romance after a hard day at work and with the kids. Buy the microwave oven and gobs of spare time will magically materialize in your busy day. Apply for a credit card and you and your children will live more interesting lives. Learn to cope with heartbreak, with dandruff and difficult bosses. Learn to balance your career and family life, personal needs and the needs of your spouse. Juggle your priorities, survive the holidays, manage your finances . . . and teach your children how to read before they're born so they don't fall behind.

But with all this great advice, things don't seem to improve substantially. We may smell better, consolidate our credit card payments and cope with cellulite while, in fact, the overall quality of our life stays put. Why? At least one contributing factor is that these very same sources that are offering us solutions would feel a negative economic impact if we actually did something that ended our stress, strain and struggle.

You, yourself, can support my point. Think of a time when you were perfectly happy. Perhaps you were sitting in front of the fire, playing with your child. Maybe you had just made it to the top of a mountain. Now, tell me. Were you counting the number of rooms in your house? Concerned about body odor?

People who are content consume less, and consume more wisely; they have fewer needs to fill. Stated another way: companies not only market to our needs . . . they market to our neediness. They know that an unhappy women is a consuming woman. And whether they are cultivating this phenomenon consciously or not, it is to their distinct advantage that we stay this way.

That's why they present us with ideals that are impossible to attain. In fact, when it looks as though we might actually attain our goals, the stakes are raised. I realized this recently while watching a documentary on the life of Marilyn Monroe. With all the jogging and dieting we've been doing, twenty-five years later—and better late than never—many of us could actually fit into a pair of her jeans. (Well, many of *you*, at any rate.) That's the good news. The bad news is that, taking a look at Marilyn now, she looks positively chubby. That is, in comparison to the models who hold forth on the pages of today's magazines . . . anorexic and eighteen. You've undoubtedly read the stories about Princess Diana looking at pictures of herself in newspapers after the birth of her second son. I don't know. She looked fine to me.

But she reportedly became "obsessed" with losing more weight. The stakes keep rising—even a princess feels inadequate. We keep crying, trying and buying.

Offering the benefit of the doubt, I do not believe there is conscious evil intent behind this—just oceans of unconsciousness. We have all been mass-hypnotized—retailers, royalty and ordinary consumers alike—with society's "watch the Rolex, watch the Rolex" thinking.

As a marketing professional, I have been on both the giving and receiving ends. Even today, I see in my bathroom cabinet not one, not two, but three—count them—three kinds of mousses. Each was purchased from one hairdresser or another, as I looked in the salon mirror at the result of hours of professional care, praying for something—anything—that might give me that same kind of lift at home. As my hairdresser—an honest man who refused to sell me yet another can—told me, in his opinion "mousse is mousse." What we have here is, even in the case of a professional marketeer like myself who should know better, a kind of mousse mentality: thinking that has been programmed, set in place and combed through by the media.

Programmed thinking is what we are faced with when, seemingly out of nowhere, we are grabbed by terror over the realization that we've forgotten to jog that morning. Not only that morning, in fact, but your entire life. Until that very moment, it had been perfectly all right with you that you hadn't jogged. Then wham! Failure City.

What was it? Piece by piece, if you so choose, you can reconstruct the influences that led to that moment. At least, the conscious ones. Your friend Sandy, who dominated the women's group last week with her tales of triumph as she crossed the finish line of the Bay to Breakers. The article you read in the local paper, reporting on some study or other that revealed women who jog regularly have happier marriages, more successful careers and fewer illnesses. What you will have more difficulty ferreting out are the ubiquitous subconscious influences. The commercial showing a couple sharing a diet drink in ecstasy while wearing jogging suits. The Nikes hanging casually from a hook in your boss's office.

The thing that is so insidious about programming is that it always exploits some basic need in reality that makes one susceptible. As hypnotists know, you can't force anyone to do anything that runs contrary to their basic inclinations. And so, at the root of jogging there may be the very healthy desire to become more physically fit. Your body wants to move, to exercise. But does your body specifically, particularly, want to jog?

Think back over your own personal history. Were you the one who in junior high school starred on the girls' track team? Or were you, like me, faking bursitis of the knees to get out of running long block?

Most of the way through my teens and twenties, I spent nary a moment feeling inadequate over the fact that I did not enjoy running. Those decades were the golden years for those of us who have spent our thirties feeling guilty because we do not jog. At that time, runners were generally thought of as some kind of cult. Major running races at best received a line in the paper. When people moved their legs frontward and backward in rapid fashion, they were doing so despite hostile looks from the occupants of passing vehicles. Running fanatics. That's how most of us passed the sixties— thinking of runners as counterculture athletes.

Then, something changed. The country became more health-conscious. Even I became more health-conscious. For one thing, the major bulk of the population was aging— the post–World War II boom babies were moving through their twenties and into cellulite, wrinkles and a "scoche more room" in their Levi's. There were new warnings on additives in our food; new research on the positive effects of diet and exercise on our health. I remember sitting face to face with my doctor who perused my extra poundage with the look of a horse trader. "If you don't exercise, you will have a body ten years older than your chronological age."

At the exact moment I was discovering that I wanted to begin exercising, the media burst into flame over jogging. The media are always on the lookout for what's next, and jogging filled the bill. Like a snowball, the cult began rolling, pushed along by the mittens of the media. At some point or other, whether the media was creating the interest or the interest creating the media craze becomes an almost Zen-like question, kind of like the chicken and the egg. (In this case, however, we're talking *poulet* and Fabergé.) In any case, the line on the famous race became a paragraph, then an article, then a whole page. As public relations agency to one of the world's largest and most popular foot races for several years, we joined in watching whole pages turn into whole newspaper supplements, live coverage on radio and television, even network news exposure. And the merchandising: designer posters, tee shirts, visors. The official beer, the official water. Our job was to make sure that all the people with the ability to move themselves from one place to another by any means possible, feel that jogging is the epitome of human expression. There were features on grandmothers who run, on families who run together, on couples who got married at the finish line. We offered advice on getting yourself up to speed to run, on what shoes to wear when you run, on what to eat for supper the night before you run.

Tens of thousands of runners. A veritable ocean of runners! The peak human experience—celebrated, reported, canonized throughout the world . . . and we were the public relations agency that shared the glory of this triumph. From cult to phenonenon!

And I? What was my part in all of this?

I felt inadequate.

I felt inadequate because I do not like to run. I did not, I still don't and I probably never will. Although during this period of several years I bought the top-of-the-line running shoes, an adorable jogging suit and a Walkman. The Walkman, I finally realized, had been a last-ditch effort to drown out the pain and discomfort with blaring music. I tried Sousa, I tried the Rolling Stones, I even tried punk.

I was still the kid who would go to any extreme to get out of running the long block.

What did not occur to me at the time was that, while I did not like jogging, there were many other things I enjoyed doing. At summer camp, I loved canoeing and rowing. Archery was terrific. And there had been a fencing class in high school I adored. In college, I folk-danced. Ballet was terrific, too, the kind of ballet I would do while no one was watching—*Swan Lake* with myself, the most graceful ballerina who ever played my living room floor, dying with the best of them.

None of this occurred to me as, trudging around my new long block in my fancy shoes, I developed the idea that if I did not jog, I could not be physically fit.

This, my friends, is programmed thinking. The kind of horse blinder mentality that keeps us miserable. I know, now, that had there been as many articles on rowing as there were on jogging, I would have found my way back to paddle and oar—and to physical-fitness ecstasy for myself—years ago. But this simply did not occur to me. It was not an option.

What I now know is that there is always an option to programmed thinking, and that is creative thinking. But creative thinking takes courage, energy and strength. It also takes awareness. Reading between the lines of commercials and the media, to separate the value to you as an individual of what is being offered from the insinuations that permeate our mass culture today: that to have a happy life, you need their product.

I have sat, unobserved and unheard, on the other side of a one-way mirror, watching consumers discuss the elements behind their decision to purchase a chocolate chip cookie. The scene went something like this:

Consumer 1: I like this one a lot. I like the taste of real butter.

Behind the mirror: *Real butter, that's a laugh. Butter-like flavor? Take a note, Lucille.*

Consumer 1: The chocolate's delicious, too. Tastes imported.

Behind the mirror: *Yeah, from the Bronx.*

Consumer 2: Well, maybe I should disqualify myself. I know this cookie. I love this cookie. I always treat myself to one when I've had problems with my boss. And I grab them between appointments, when there isn't time for lunch.

Behind the mirror: *Now she's talking. We can do something with that. Make a note, Lucille. Problems, that's good.*

The panel tasting the chocolate chip cookies was heavily weighted with women. So are other such panels on product categories ranging from dish detergent to potato chips, from car seat covers to household appliances.

When it comes to purchasing things, women hold the dominant influence in a great number of categories. Women are also the major subscribers to life-style magazines and the major purchasers of books. And it is for these women, in great part, that advertising developed the fine art of life-style messages. Unlike advertisements presenting practical information on product quality and ingredients, life-style advertising presents an emotional portrait of what your life could be like if you were to use the product. That's why we have beverage ads with legions of tap-dancing sophisticates hoofing through the streets in a joyous celebration of life. And you are not sure, when finished, whether the rhapsodic nectar is cola or root beer. We are asked to use catalogs that will mysteriously land us in some handsome man's apartment, buy underwear that somehow holds the promise of a ménage à trois.

Like an archeologist who finally cracked the hieroglyphic

code, I feverishly turned the pages of the stack of helpful women's magazines I kept in my bedside stand. Through the years of my superwoman mania, they had been a prime source of support. I turned to them when I chose to put my son in daycare—praying that they would say it's okay. I clipped recipes that I could prepare in the two minutes I had each evening between the time I walked in the door exhausted, and one or more of my family members began crying that they were starved. With my new clarity of vision, I recognized a complex interplay of advertising and editorial copy that helped keep us stuck in our programming. Virtually every article offered advice on various ways to deal with the stresses and strains of our lives. Editorial copy soothingly assured us that with their sage knowledge, drawn from the top psychologists, educators and home economists in the world, we could learn to cope quite nicely.

As the word about my organization hits the media, it has been gratifying to see that among those addressing the issues we are raising there have been a wide range of women's magazines. I can see the willingness and the necessity to respond to our growing awareness, an impulse already manifesting itself in the editorial content of many of the publications quoted in these next two chapters. Advertising, too, is coming along. As we speak out, we can have impact on our world. If we remain silent, however, the world will continue to have impact on us.

Take one single issue of *Working Mother* magazine as an example. Dated December, 1985, this issue is now history—the kind of history that has made us who we are today.

In large red type, the front-cover headline reads, HAVE IT ALL FOR THE HOLIDAYS!

The ad inside the front cover is for Cover Girl Moisture Wear Makeup. It consists of an exquisite full-color, full-page photo of a perfect pink rose, and the copy reads, "Moisture. It keeps this flower fresh and beautiful all day."

On the inside back cover, a dashing woman in a black Fedora hat picks a cigarette out from the pack by her teeth, under the headline, DARE TO BE MORE.

So there you are, superwomen circa mid-1980s . . . you haven't even gotten to the body of the magazine, and you've already received three major messages to the effect that, by reading the articles, using this makeup and smoking this cigarette you can have it all, stay fresh and beautiful all day and still dare to be more.

You, meanwhile, are stuck in traffic, the only time you can find for yourself, watching over your shoulder so that the policeman doesn't catch you reading at the wheel.

"You'll find that we're the one magazine that understands *you*. Because you're more than just a trendy life-style. You're a working mother."

A trendy life-style? Perish the thought, officer. I've got major issues to deal with— Yes! Send me the next twelve volumes. Particularly the one that will answer the question, "Do you *really* know what to do with styling mousse? We have regular beauty/fashion features for the woman who has little time for herself."

And no wonder—she is exhausting herself trying to have it all for the holidays.

As I said in the last chapter, it's better to know how to cope than not to. But isn't it time to stop reassuring one another that we're "happy and fulfilled," that we have just these few little problems—"sometimes."

Let's face it. We're miserable. Off the deep end. I've got thousands of letters from judges, factory workers, housewives and career women whose minds were never crossed by the thought that they might be "just a trendy life-style." They have fears and conflicts beyond what even Whirlpool's new TimeMaster microwave oven can handle, because "these days, you're probably finding less and less time to prepare delicious meals. . . . Quick Defrost gets meals ready faster than before. . . . So a meal that took ten minutes to thaw now only takes six."

Well, Whirlpool, every bit helps.

Defrost two or three meals a day, and you might even save enough time for *Self* magazine's "Fifteen-minute Energy Renewers" (November, 1985).

"Suddenly you're all pooped out—with lots more to do and a big night ahead. Here's how to revive."

To the rescue: mind and body exercises for stress reduction.

Fifteen minutes will "rekindle your zip and spirit fast."

Everybody eagerly reads the exercises . . . but nobody questions why you are running day and night, in the first place.

Then, there's Jane Fonda. Fifteen minutes? You've got to be kidding. Jane's experiences, reported in newspapers across the country, "are that people who are healthier with a greater aerobic fitness have an expanded ability to engage in other activities. . . ." (*USA Weekend,* November 15–17, 1985).

Expanded ability? Like to get the laundry folded before midnight? Finish the PTA newsletter before the semester ends? Get the children the allergy shots, and not get laid off for excessive absenteeism?

No . . . Jane means activities like "dancing, hiking, volleyball, softball."

But first, to get to this golden mecca, the "sophisticated exerciser" takes Jane's advice . . .

"Five years ago, you would find a woman who would come to an aerobics class anywhere from four to six times a week. Now she may come three times a week."

That's some kind of progress . . . but wait. Jane continues . . .

"And, in addition, she works with free weights or circuit training two or three times a week and may also run."

After all this, the November, 1985 issue of *Ladies' Home Journal* hits home when it asks in its headline story, "Doctor, Why Am I So Tired?"

"Ever feel dizzy or just plain exhausted? This expert explains why—and offers simple remedies."

Eagerly devoured reading—althought it takes toothpicks to keep my lids open after a busy day taking the kids to school and daycare, going to work, doing the shopping, making dinner, balancing the checkbook and planning strategies with my husband for the next day's obligations. No time for aerobics or softball. The article is five pages long. The root of all the problems of the decade is nutritional deficiency. We're talking vitamins and minerals—five pages' worth.

Everywhere you look—newspapers, magazines, television—you are given helpful advice. For improved self-esteem, manicure your nails. For stress, try the B vitamins. But for God's sake, your family's sake and your credit card company's sake—keep coping, keep going, keep your upper lip so stiff you end up looking like a camel.

Rarely, however, is the most logical answer to the question, "Why am I so tired?" even hinted at.

In my humble, noncredentialed opinion, perhaps the reason you are always so tired is that you are always trying to do too much.

This basic truth is the great sacred cow for women in the 80s, who are afraid to tell the truth on this matter, and when they do tell it, they get little support for doing so from either advertising or editorial copy. And, what's even sadder to tell, for the most part not even from one another—from the role models of our generation.

_____*Chapter Four*_____

ROLE-ING RIGHT ALONG

The story always goes like this. Mrs. Big Star, career in full
bloom, young children and faltering marriage, used to have
problems coping. She used to have trouble fitting everything in. However, by the time you're reading about her in
the newspaper, she's always licked her [choose one or more]
cocaine habit/alcoholism/breakdown. She did so through
[choose as many as can fit in the space of the article] medita-
tion/exercise/judicious consumption of vegetables/help
from a new husband/help from a therapist/from the Betty
Ford Center.

Now, as you read about the new, improved version, Mrs.
Star has made huge changes. Her career is booming, her
children are delighted with mommy's success, her marriage
is working and she has a whole contingent of spiritual, psychological and physical regimens. In fact, Mrs. Star is so

busy now that she's learned to do the things that help her cope, juggle and balance, that she doesn't appear to have time to enjoy any of it.

Take the Nashville-datelined interview with a well known country star that ran in newspapers across the country. The journalist writes of the star's life being "back in balance" with the degree of suspension of judgment otherwise reserved for heroines of romance novels. In this case, the star's multiple-choice selection came out to be cocaine.

But, the author hurries to assure us, "balancing family and career needs isn't something the once anxious mother finds difficult anymore."

"That's my full-time job," the FDA-approved star says of her youngsters. And singing? "That's my part-time job. No, actually, I have two full-timers."

She goes on to admit that "it takes a tremendous amount of energy to balance it."

But balance it, we are assured in headline type, she does.

Artists, by definition, are exceptional people. One has no doubt that in the process of creating her albums, this star— as she is quoted—opened the space for exploring the feelings and emotions involved with such challenges as a "marital shake-up and battle for abstinence." She describes her album as a "catharsis for her emotional trauma." In a personal conflict over how much to reveal, she finally agrees that the best art is one that strikes the deepest emotional response.

"If you wanna do that, I guess you've got to give a lot away."

So why do we have here, in the pages of newspapers across the country, this blood-and-guts woman assuring us that it is not difficult for her to balance family and career now? Why are the celebrity's problems in this archetypal, sanitized media story always in the past? Why does this star present herself as finally "having it all together" while her fans struggle to balance the complexities of career and family? They are given a role model who claims to have time to do everything—and still get to bed early. More women will undoubtedly read about this star and those like her than will hear her album. So what use is it to bare her soul for art if then all she does in print is pontificate that "if I'm centered and if I'm in the right frame of mind then everything else will fall into line."

"If" is one thing. The road to reality, however, can often take more than a few bumpy turns. We all know the stories about famous political wives whose faces "blossomed with an unusual serenity" that turned out, in retrospect, to be induced by heavy doses of tranquilizers. This breed of role model is always emerging from a difficult year "with humor and candor intact."

But how many times can one overcome difficulties and emerge intact? One can't help but wonder how it is that all the women who have been so idolized in the media during our formative years—and well into the present—have rarely been caught at an inopportune moment.

Playgirl magazine's "Ten Most Admired Women" of 1985 (December, 1985) all shared the same purple headline . . . TODAY, THE WOMEN WE ADMIRE MOST ARE INDEPENDENT, SUCCESSFUL REBELS WHO HAVE COPED WITH ADVERSITY.

People like Mary Tyler Moore who "in the last five years [has] become her own woman, breaking through a lifelong reserve, overcoming a plague of personal tragedies and emerging triumphant."

Playgirl assures us that this is the year that "women no longer have to strive. They have already arrived. . . . Now that women have proven they can do anything, it's how they do it that counts. As we looked around, we saw admirable women making their own way on their own terms, the best kind of role models for all."

Not one of the role models in the article appears to be

currently struggling with the conflict between career and family or to be having problems trying to fit everything in. Take Sally Field. She may have won two Oscars, but "the role she feels most comfortable in [is] mother to her two teenage sons by an early marriage. Her hands-on role includes carpooling, cleaning, cooking, grocery shopping and all the other 'ings' mothers do."

She may feel most comfortable doing motherly ings, but she has somehow found the time to found a film production company and make a romantic comedy in which she costars with James Garner.

It's not just the famous who oblige the media with "boundless energy" and the belief "that we could do anything we wanted, providing we worked hard enough for it" (Donna Zaccaro, speaking of the kind of role model her mother, Geraldine Ferraro, was for her—*McCall's*, November, 1985).

In my hometown newspaper a search for special people, run in conjunction with a major department store chain, resulted in this copy.

"There never seems to be enough time in the day to do just the routine things, let alone the extras. . . . Then there are the special people, those who—no matter how busy—find the time to go the extra mile. And look as fresh and stylish as though they didn't have a thing to do all day except get dressed."

Take one of the examples, the parents of a one-year-old child who "managed to maintain a balanced relationship and cohesive family unit, all the while producing three publications between them."

And then there is that article hanging on the wall of my conference room about the businesswoman who "used to have trouble balancing all the pieces, but now has her priorities straight again" . . . and again and again.

That would be me.

One of those inspiring women entrepreneurs. Always triumphing over incredible odds to start this or that company or project. Supportive husband, offering quotes about how "terrific a wife and mother she is. She somehow manages to do it all." Throwing off children as quickly and easily as flapjacks from the pan. And still has time to exercise, volunteer, vacation in Europe and sit on a board or two.

Okay, okay. So I left a couple of little things out. Like the fact that my son had a never-ending string of ear infections, related in some way to unspecific allergies that the doctor offered "might be stress-related." Like the fact I sometimes came home from work, threw cartons of Chinese food on the dinner table and went to bed in a puddle of inexplicable tears. Like the Maalox, bought in case lots. Like the feeling of complete and utter hopelessness that swept over me at unpredictable intervals—at times when I should have been happiest.

Like when the journalist was asking me my secret of success. I realized the awesome responsibility of being singled out as a woman who was making a contribution, and I didn't want to blow it for myself or other women by telling the whole truth. After all, I knew how hard we—and the women who blazed the trail before us—have fought for what we have. We have courageously opened up careers that had formerly been male strongholds. We have navigated the waters of politics, education and the arts—exploring financial and professional vistas previously beyond the reach of women. We have chosen to have children—consciously promising our mates, bosses and mothers that we were up to whatever challenges lay ahead. Was I going to sit here now and whine about it, particularly when I knew, in the secret recesses of my heart, that if I was having difficulty getting it together it must be my own fault. Something I just hadn't quite gotten down. If Sally Field could do it, why couldn't I? Would I have to be the first to say, "Hey, I don't seem to be making it on my own terms. I don't seem to be able to prove I can do everything!"

Instead, my voice was added to the litany of role models; the exposure generated the admiration of my peers, new business leads and—inexplicably—it prompted at the same time a growing sense of personal betrayal. The division between the public perception of myself and the private recognition that all was not well was growing.

I sat before more clients than I would like to admit, laundering the answer to the question, "How are you?" with enough soap powder to bubble up the Pacific Ocean. When you are face-to-face with the person who pays your salary, you do some pretty funny things. Like pretend you were home sick when, in truth, you were attending your child's school play. Or tell them you need to leave for a board meeting promptly at 5 P.M. *Black*board, that is—the one in your son's daycare center.

This is fear—merited in many cases—that if we admit publicly the strain we are under, our hard-won gains will be taken away. Feeling that we should buck up, no matter the stress we are under, like good professionals marching to the economic wars. And women have been good soldiers. Good soldiers with husbands who want tasty dinners, children with homework to do—all on top of our challenging careers. Careers that we got in the first place by trying harder, working longer, charging less and being better than our male competitors—position by hard-won position, job by job.

Stars are equally vulnerable. For them, the mere hint that they may not have it all together could bring with it rumors of instability and flakiness—risks producers and promoters don't particularly want to take. They sell their tickets on the promise of delivering the mind, soul and body of the artist to the concert hall or movie screen.

Unfortunately, some of our women celebrities roll onto the success wagon cozily ensconced in a world of British-trained nannies and French cooks, pulling up the ladder after themselves. They, as much as anybody, become defenders of the myth. Their buttoned-down success story becomes a bad habit. Imagine how ridiculous they will look as, woman by woman, we realize that the ideals they represent are simply too good to be true.

As in the story of the Emperor's new clothes, we can each be the little boy who was unafraid to state the obvious—the boy who finally got up the nerve to declare publicly what everyone in the kingdom privately knew: the Emperor had no clothes. He was stark naked, in fact.

In circle after circle of friends, one by one, women are taking the risk to whisper the truth about their lives to each other. Selena Dixon, a geologist with a major oil company and a mother of two, wrote to tell me, "I realized I can't have it all. Something had to be sacrificed. I was not happy as a superwoman. I have not met anyone who will admit this to me."

Now Selena is out in the open, affecting the currents of public opinion in her community in ever-growing circles.

And thank heavens. For by not telling the truth to each other for so long, women have been divided, isolated. If there was even a chance to come together publicly to flex our newfound economic muscle, to make changes, we never found it.

We were either one of the special people or one of the inadequate ones—with our personal secrets to be hidden at all costs.

The cost to me of going public was real. When I finally spoke out, declared myself to be one who had had "enough," rumors of pending bankruptcy started circulating. The fact that profitability was up at our agency, that we had, in fact, dropped "in" to something richer, not "out" of it, took many months to surface.

The real cost was the years—and the deeply ingrained

tendency in our culture to avoid pain at any cost. The desire to stay safe, protected and secret with our vulnerability— stuck in a life-style that doesn't work due, in part, to our unwillingness to be real with each other and with ourselves. Stuck in the belief that there is something more we can have, do or be that will make the difference.

PART II.

Drive Yourself to Happiness

_____Chapter Five_____

TO DO OR NOT TO DO

The parts of this handbook I like best are the ones that point the finger of blame in any direction other than mine. It's the economy's fault, for instance. Or that of previous generations.

However, the problem with maintaining this point of view for too long is that, as terrific as it feels at the time, there's not a whole heck of a lot any of us can do about generations that have already come and gone or even about the economy, for that matter. That's the bad news.

The good news is that there _is_ something we can do a whole heck of a lot about. That would be, simply, how we choose to live our lives. You know you have the ability to change how you do things, otherwise you'd still be sucking baby bottles. You probably have the motivation, as well, otherwise you probably would have put this handbook down and gone to make a phone call to the office to see what you've been missing during the past three paragraphs.

I don't want to spoil all our fun, however. So let's take a moment to have a good pout over how unfair life is. Think about all the terrible things those bad, bad people have done to us. They have, you know.

Okay. Put the hanky away. We've got an experiment to do.

Experiment Number One: Busyness

Setup

Are you interested, fascinated or scared to find out why you are always running? You won't need to consult your memogenda for this one.

In just five minutes' time, if you promise to do what I ask, you can find the answer. But what I am going to ask you to do may be very difficult. For many, it will prove impossible.

You will be tempted to cheat by cutting the experiment short. Perhaps you will go as far as to pretend to yourself, "I have already done it once," or "That's a dumb idea."

These are all avoidance tactics. Do the experiment, then come back to read the analysis.

The Experiment

Do nothing for five full minutes.

Analysis

There is a qualitative difference between spending time, investing time, even wasting time—and doing nothing. If you were even able to do the experiment at all, you probably found doing five minutes of nothing somewhere on the scale between uncomfortable and excruciating.

You may have noticed your mind racing from one obligation to another; your body may have felt awkward. Maybe you fell asleep.

Interestingly, the one quality we want more of in our superpaced lives is serenity. We want the kind of strength that truly great and powerful women exude. Stability.

When superwomen get quiet with themselves, they also come face-to-face with their center. Not the serene core we'd hoped to encounter but, more often than not, a center of turbulence. Rather than stay with it, explore it, experiment with it, make friends with it, we often run in the opposite direction, down the path of least resistance. Busyness. I don't think that it is completely accidental that "busyness" looks an awful lot like "business." But there are lots of ways to keep busy—and superwomen do them all. Here is a rundown of superwomen styles. Which one is yours?

Magna Mater

She is a terrific mother. Loves her children. She makes all their clothes. For Halloween she created a pumpkin costume—complete with flashing light bulbs for the eyes. Little Michael was hysterical because he would have preferred to go as one of those Smurfs that come out of a box at the five-and-dime. But never mind.

She's the one who flourished when her children were in their climbing stage. She invented this great shelf system so that the kids could reach the appropriate toys without disturbing her fine breakables. There's a separate box for every size and shape of Tinkertoy.

Then Michael went to kindergarten. Magna Mater was devastated. She walked him to the front door of his classroom every day, finding all sorts of excuses to run back home and bring him a forgotten item for show-and-tell. But there was something dangerous creeping into her life. Free time. She had things handled. Her life was balanced.

Meet her solution: Jessica Ann, now seven months old—and what a handful.

The Boss

She's got her life *organized*. Every possibility, every contingency—at the office or at home—is handled. Of course they would be. She's using the same set of skills that got her out of the secretarial pool and into the corner office in the first place.

Child is miserable teething? Organize it.

Husband feeling lonely? Organize that as well.

She's dynamic. She's wonderful. Making her million-dollar deal in Denver on Monday, wowing them at the sales conference on Tuesday, presenting her report to the Board of Directors on Wednesday. You say there is a message on her desk. Husband and child just left on a cruise for "Parents without Partners?"

Call the housekeeper. Tell her to take the roast out of the oven. Good news! The Boss can work late tonight!

The Seeker

Poor Mary. She knows her life is missing something. She's already quit her job. The kids are handled. The husband is supportive. Now she's going to find herself.

From 6:30 to 7:30 A.M., dream analysis. From 7:30 to 8:30 A.M., aerobics. 8:30 to 8:35 A.M., quality time with the children as they leave for school. 8:35 to 9:30, read a self-help book. 9:30 to 10:00 A.M., get dressed (preferably in something made of cotton, and on the baggy side). 10:00 A.M. to 1:00 P.M., women's brown-bag group. 1:00 P.M. to 2:00 P.M., private session of neurolinguistics. 2:00 to 5:00 P.M., class at junior college: creative expression sampler. 5:00 to 6:00 P.M., cast the I Ching. 6:00 to 6:30 P.M., dinner with family. 6:30 to 7:30 P.M., journal about the day's activities. 7:30 to 11:00 P.M., consciousness seminar.

But something is still missing. Mary finally figures it out. What she wants more than anything is a richer relationship with her husband and children.

She knows just what to do. Remember that home-study videotape on how to have terrific relationships that the bookstore just got in? There must be some time she can fit that in. Maybe instead of dinner. Her family will understand.

The Volunteer

Need somebody to do something? Ask Joan. She works at the charity thrift shop, edits the information booklet for the PTA and serves as chairman of the Church's fund-raising committee.

She's got plenty of time with her family. She sees her husband at the start of the parade just before the float he built for the booster club that she heads up takes off. She sees her children every day—as crossing guard. "Hi, Ginnie! Hi, Tom!"

As a tutor, she's taught hundreds of people to read. Too bad she doesn't have the time to open the book she could hardly wait to get out of the library—which she manages two mornings a week.

Joan is the one the other mothers call when they are too busy at the office to get their kids after school. She's also the one who feels bad because she isn't working.

And then there's me (and, I suspect, you). I have managed Magna Mater, the Boss, the Seeker and the Volunteer simultaneously. Down to the pumpkin costume.

This kind of busyness—this maniacal life-style—is a kind of drug. First you like it, then you get used to it, then you need it. Geared up all the time—dealing with things, organizing pieces, making schedules. It is a socially acceptable drug, in a society where people define themselves by what they do and have, not by who they are. In fact, the motto of our society could easily be—with apologies to Descartes—"I do, therefore I am."

You love your children? How do you show it? In our culture, you demonstrate the quality of your love by the number of classes you are willing to drag them to. Baby is loved if the outfit she is wearing was bought at I. Magnin's. She is *really* loved if it was hand-knitted.

In our society we don't just have love, we earn it. We do our part, pitch in. If you really love me, you'll carry out the garbage.

We judge ourselves by what we are willing to do for each other.

"She's my best friend. She is the one I can count on to take the kids overnight when we need to go away on business."

And we judge each other by what we have.

"They're doing fabulously. Did you hear they just got a new Mercedes—picked it up in Germany!"

We value ourselves by our roles. In many communities, status comes from combining work and motherhood. (And God forbid anybody should find out you don't make your child's oatmeal from scratch.)

In other communities, the sign of status is to not have to work. In these suburban enclaves, working mothers are sniffed upon in observance of some kind of quaint, tribal custom. "Isn't it cute, that you work."

Mothers who work bend over backward to prove their children are getting all the advantages. Mothers who don't work bend over backward to prove they have capabilities to make things happen in the "real world" too.

Career women are reluctant to get sufficient household help, retaining some or all of the key "woman's role" jobs for themselves. Sweep your own floor, diaper your own baby, cook your own goose, for that matter—try to prove to your husband that you are a woman first, the president of some corporation second.

Everybody is busy proving something to somebody. It's intoxicating. And it distracts us from the uncomfortable feelings we have when we pause for a moment, just as a drug would. This kind of busyness, the frenzied lives we choose to lead, lets us gloss over those feelings—and ourselves.

Over lunch—when we finally get together—we think we are being real with each other. Baring all. We complain about how busy we are. Share tips on good sitters. Talk about our latest triumphs at work, our children's successes in school. Don't forget the update on vacations, material possessions and awards. When we've run out of all these, we talk about dieting.

Stay ten pounds overweight. That's a great way to stay busy. You can make a career of it, as a matter of fact. Whatever free time you might otherwise have had, you can spend at diet classes, reading diet books, cooking up strange diet concoctions.

Overeating is another great way to stay busy.

Then, when you get together with your friends, you can create the illusion of intimacy by moaning to them over all the reasons the latest diet didn't work.

The illusion of intimacy. One of the best friends of busyness. Entertaining your spouse—holding hands in public, sipping an expensive wine in the best restaurants. Everybody thinks you are madly in love. Then, whoops. Out of nowhere, he's taken up with another woman.

Did *you* think you were in love? Did you forget to think? Too busy to look?

And your friends. Are you sure they would be there for you if you stopped coping? They can barely make it to lunch. Would you ask them for help? Or would you rather discuss the relative merits of Weight Watchers versus the Diet Center?

When our lives are built on what we do and have, built on proving our worth to each other on the basis of the roles we hold, there is no stability—no center or base.

And when the center does not hold, we literally threaten to come unglued. So what is the logical thing for a woman in this situation to try? Right. Do something about it.

Doing things, however, is the problem. So the harder we try to do things that will fix our lives, the worse things get.

Our engines get overrevved. You know the sinking feeling. We are hysterically trying to catch up, and things keep getting worse. The car stalls, your appointment stands you up, you get a phone call from the school nurse telling you to pick up your child. And then your mother calls to ask you how you are doing.

The next time you go into overdrive, just stop. Don't think about the problem, think about nothing. Now, I know what you're saying. You're already behind and sinking deeper, and you should lose another five minutes doing nothing? But think about it, there are 288 five-minute segments in a day, 2,016 in a week, and if you are thirty-five years old, over three and a half million have passed by already. If you are already going under, taking an infinitesimal fraction of your life to try something different is not going to be the thing that finally does you in. And it could open up a whole new world of possibilities.

Possibilities? Out of doing nothing for five minutes? When I was studying karate, my sensei told me a story that holds a clue as to how this might be so.

A student went to study with a Zen master. He began by telling the master how hard he had worked to arrive at this moment. The master invited him for tea. As the student talked about his accomplishments, the master poured tea into his cup. The cup became full, and then it began to overflow. The master kept pouring.

"Master! Stop! Can't you see . . . you are spilling tea everywhere?"

The master stopped and looked at the student. "That's just my point. You can't pour tea into a cup that is already full."

_____*Experiment Number Two*_____

Do experiment number one again—do nothing for five full minutes. But this time, I'm going to help you out. Make sure you carefully study the following page.

_____*Gift from My Childhood*_____

When I was just about Grant's age, six or seven years old, I sent a message to my adult self. It arrived not so long ago, inexplicably one evening as I lay exhausted on the sofa. The delivery of the gift signaled the beginning of what has turned out to be the most amazing year of my life. A year of personal change beyond my wildest dreams.

It was right around Thanksgiving, 1955 or 1956. I was riding in the backseat of my family's car—a great big green Rambler. Sunshine was warming a spot next to me on the seat, and I reached out to touch it. As I wriggled my fingers in the rays, I felt completely happy. There was no particular reason—no birthday or school play—but a special moment of happiness that depended on nothing but myself.

Many years later, I recalled what I said to myself at the time. That this would be a moment I would remember forever. The child in me sent me that memory through the years, my own ray of sunshine: a softness, a brightness, an "okayness" that had nothing to do with my accomplishments or the events in my life.

I knew then, as I remember more often than not now, that there is no reason for feeling happiness.

_____*Chapter Six*_____

NOTHING BUT THE TRUTH

The economic establishment will not like the idea that I am advocating "down time" for women. That is valuable time when we could be buying and doing things that make money for other people.

Coping is much safer for everybody. We can let the steam out by complaining to our friends about our busy schedules. We buy the microwave ovens and perfume, and nothing ever changes. Maybe not appreciably for the better—but usually, at least, also not for the worse.

In fact, it is the fear that change might shake the status quo into a downturn that keeps us playing the game. We are afraid that, if we turn off the external programming and start to look into our own hearts for direction, we might like what we find even less. As if our inner recesses were cheap lodgings for some huge, slothful creature that is big, hairy and has exceedingly bad breath.

Upon describing some of the colorful beasts in my own reservoir of fear, one sympathetic friend of mine—an anthropologist—had the tact to comment that my thinking on this matter was "primitive." Primitive or not, it took me thirty years or so before I realized that the value of looking inward was worth the risk of what I might uncover. I was terrified that what I might find out about myself—some psychological or spiritual malfunction—would be truly horrible. After years of serious exploration of my inner recesses, I am sorry to report that it was worse than that. What I found were not uncontrollable horrors of mystical origin, but rather things that I could do something about. I expected black holes and gremlins. Instead, I discovered that I had a sinking feeling that one of my employees was making a habit of coming in late every day. Dark holes I could have spent years in therapy for. The employee I had to see today.

I would rather eat ten ice-cream sundaes than confront somebody. They could get angry and hit me. Or cry. Or, horrors, accuse me of pointing the finger at them falsely. A whole host of yucky things. I'd take a black hole—with bad breath, even—any day.

Sadly enough, if you don't look at the issues, they are still there, doing things like coming in late to work. You may busily breeze in and out of your office, even bid a cheery good morning to the Issue, but somewhere—down deep—you know. It's worth a couple of candy bars to keep one like that in abeyance for a while. In fact, one clue that your subconscious might be on to something, is that revving up response discussed earlier. Your pace is speeding up and you are absolutely certain that this is not the time you could possibly take five minutes for yourself. This is a sure sign that there's something cooking that you don't want to look at. We call this the Tooth Fairy Theory of Problem Management. You are hoping that, through some magical means external to yourself, if you stall long enough, the problem will go away.

Tell the truth. With the one exception, years ago, when the boyfriend you were finally getting up enough courage to leave came to see you on his own accord to say, "I'm sorry, but I've got another girl," this does not happen often.

That is reality.

Reality is not a subject that bona fide superwomen know much about. On the simplest level, superwomen have trouble with such concepts as the fact that there are twenty-four hours in a day, that you can't be in two places at the same time, and that when your gas gauge is empty, the car will stop.

Want some proof that you are literally out of touch with reality?

Experiment Number Three

Setup

If you are like most women today, you feel inadequate because you cannot accomplish all the tasks in your life with ease and effortlessness.

You may beg for, borrow or steal whatever time you can to study women's magazines for advice, self-help books and television talk shows—but have you ever asked yourself whether there are literally enough hours in the day to fit everything in? Have you, in fact, put together a life that could possibly work? Forget about prioritization and time management for a moment and take an honest look at your life. Here's the definitive experiment that will prove just how out of touch you are.

The Experiment

There are 168 hours in a week. This startlingly meager number is based on the commonly agreed upon contemporary understanding that days consist of twenty-four hours and weeks of seven days, and years of fifty-two weeks. Are we still together?

Good. Grab some scratch paper and do the following calculation. Start with 168 hours. From this, subtract the amount of time you would like to sleep each night times seven. Don't cheat by saying, as you often do, "I can get by on five hours if I have to." This number should be the proper amount to get you bounding out of the sack and doing jigs. I do understand that, at this point, you may be tempted to say, "Eighteen hours." And truth is, after cutting this area of your life so short for so long, you might need a few round-the-clockers (meals airlifted to your bedroom) to start off. For this purpose, use the average number you think you'd like after you hit some sort of equilibrium.

Now subtract the amount of time you actually spend each week at work—on the job or volunteering. Honest, now: include the work that comes home in the briefcase . . . the cakes that get baked for the sale . . . the extra trip to the post office to mail the flyers. If some of these activities come up once a year—like leading the cub scouts on a litter drive to clean up a local expressway, estimate the number of hours that takes and divide by fifty-two.

Now subtract the total amount of commute time—both directions—multiplied by the number of days you work in a week. Allow for heavy traffic and missed buses.

How much time do you think you should or would like to spend with your children and/or pets over a week's period? Pick the highest number and write that down as well.

Now, how about your mate? How many times have you vowed to spend at least a couple of nights a week out together just for fun . . . meet at the office for romantic lunches? How many hours is that? If you're not hitched, how much time do you put into being in the right place at the right time, suffering through blind dates and going to parties?

Okay, now let's think about friends. To how many of them have you said, "Let's get together soon"? How many hours would it take in a week if you actually carried through with it—or already do!

Okay, now get ready for a biggie. How much time should you be spending on physical exercise? Remember that three-mornings-a-week aerobics class you've resolved to start? Include the time it would take to change, drive and shower.

Chores around the house: shopping, laundry, unexpected repairs. How's that 168 hours a week looking?

How about the time it would take for you to look great every day? How much time would you spend washing up in the morning, applying your makeup, that clay facial you've had sitting on your shelf for a year?

Add in however much time it takes to do your hair yourself, or however often you go to the hairdressers, and divide it down into a week's period.

Haven't you always meant to journalize, or read that book that's sitting on your bedside stand? Are your subscriptions piling up? How many *Wall Street Journals* behind are you now? What would it take to keep up with these simple pleasures?

How about a special treat, occasionally? A massage, an afternoon walking on a favorite hill, that class you've been meaning to get to?

Whoops, almost forgot helping with your kid's homework, visiting your parents and doing your family's bookkeeping. Taking your children to lessons and classes? Going to Church?

Any of the 168 left?

Here's the clincher. The amount of time you spend lining up baby-sitters.

I'm sure that there is more that you do in your life. Holiday and birthday preparations (divided by fifty-two, for instance).

Complete your calculations, then report back for analysis.

Analysis

How far in the hole are you? If you managed to break even, a big goose egg, that's what one would call "coping." If you're in the red, at least now you are in touch with reality. You're not inadequate—you are simply trying to do more than is humanly possible. You could do what Julius Caesar did in ancient Rome—he changed the calendar to suit his own taste. He messed with the number of days in a month, even named one month after himself. In case you are not an emperor of the known world, however, you will probably want to read on.

If you were to follow this same procedure on your budget, by the way—contrasting weekly expenditures to weekly income, you would probably find that your stay in Fantasyland does not end with the hour hand on the Mickey Mouse clock. In our pocketbooks and in our lives, we are borrowing against our own futures—which are rapidly being sold down the river by the "best and brightest" generation in history.

Once you can get your brain around the fact that there is such a thing as reality, you are ready to start telling the truth about what it is you want in your life—how you want to live.

Here's where the women's magazines are like pigs in mud. They are absolutely devoted to helping us live better lives. They do so by using one of those million-dollar words I propose to retire. *Prioritizing.* Come on, now. We're talking here to women who haven't even made peace with the fact that time passes in twenty-four-hour cycles.

Prioritization is a euphemism for "Let's pretend there's plenty of time in the day for us to do the important things, and the little things will take care of themselves later." Women's magazines tell us this because they don't want to upset us by telling us the truth.

And what is the truth? As your negative numbers from Experiment Three definitively tell you, *you cannot have it all*.

You can prioritize until the cows come home; the little things will probably not get done later. And, if you are like most superwomen, you've got too many "important" things competing for the top slots in any case.

Think of the recording artist whose life is now "back in balance." When asked about her priorities, she answered of her youngsters, "That's my full-time job." And singing? "That's my part-time job. No, actually, I have two full-timers."

If you are extremely efficient, you may even look for a solution through the study of time management. Time management, in my book, belongs on the same list as dieting and fear of furry beasts. All new and improved ways to stay busy, busy, busy. Through time management, you may create the miracle of womanhood circa mid-1980s. You may get each and every one of the pieces on your list to function perfectly. You might even, glory be, become a role model. Career's going great, kids are successful, the marriage is holding and you are living in your dream house. All the pieces are doing fine—but only you know that the pieces do not come together to make a whole. You are not happy.

The reason for this discrepancy is linear thinking. Linear thinking comes from the rational side of the brain that loves making lists—keeping things organized and controlled. This side of the brain adores prioritizing—but doesn't know beans about the quality of life. As Mr. Spock would probably say, "Quality of life is not quantifiable. If it can't be put into a computer, it does not belong on a list." Rational thought comes in very handy when you're doing things like making grocery lists. But in subjects as near to our hearts as what we want to experience for ourselves this lifetime, we had better start consulting other parts of our anatomy. Something closer to the heart. Like the side we spoke of earlier, the one that has a hard time shouting over the hubbub of our busy days making lists, fitting things in, managing time. The intuitive side, when given even the littlest bit of encouragement, is full of surprises: intuitions that pan out, dreams that hold messages, realizations that—whether you like the idea or not—you know to be true.

The intuitive side is also the caretaker of what you really want for yourself. The intuitive side understands feelings like fulfillment, self-expression and love. The intuitive side does not care two figs for the number of rooms in your house. The intuitive side does not even care if you accomplish any of the items on your list, as long as you are happy.

The economic establishment does not like the intuitive side, either.

In fact, there is virtually no support in our society today for cultivation of this amazing source of inspiration and vitality that each of us carries within. It is up to you, therefore, to make room for this quality in your own life. To declare that you are courageously freeing yourself from external programming to begin to dance to your own music. But that means telling the truth. And one of the first things you must tell the truth about is this: that whether you are living a quality life or not is your choice, completely and totally up to you.

To move from linear thinking to whole-brain thinking—giving both your rational side and your intuitive side their appropriate functions—requires a much greater talent than juggling or balancing. It requires, in fact, a leap of faith to a new way of experiencing your life. Instead of changing the pieces—working from the outside in—you will have to alter the very core. Your perceptions of individual events, people and activities will shift. Where there was once confusion and frustration, there will be clarity. Instead of a sinking feeling of inadequacy, there will be choices. This is another way of saying growth. Not linear growth: good, better, best. But a quantum leap to a new set of exciting premises. Premises that make the move from superwoman to great woman a real possibility.

Perhaps you have already felt this shift. It does not necessarily take a long time to get the concept. In fact, I've received a number of letters from women who say that merely hearing the words *enough is enough* served as a wake-up call to new perspectives. Like a hypnotic state that needs only the clapping of hands to give way to consciousness, our intuitive mind is always ready and eager to be roused from slumber.

When awakened, you will feel, at last, the potential for integrity—for a congruency in your life. You may not be there yet—but you will know what you need to get there. And more often than not, sooner or later you are willing to do it.

Whether you believe this or not is irrelevant. Whether this is true or not is also irrelevant. If you follow the steps in this handbook, you will begin to practice your own innate ability to start living your own life. That's the nice part. The part we would rather not hear about is what we will have to call up from ourselves to do so: courage.

For some, the safe harbor of coping, juggling and balancing may be the preferred way to go. Each one of us always has the option of keeping things the way they are: including the complaining. Even the most skeptical among you could try ideas out in this book for a while, feeling secure that you can always exercise the option of getting your old life back.

In fact, at any given moment or day, I may be right in there with you. To make changes, you do need courage. And even then, there can be scary moments. I offer my family's "dream house" as a prime example. For fifteen years—since the day Dan and I first met—we shared the fantasy of living in an incredible house together some day. On one early anniversary, I gave Dan a gift subscription to *Architectural Digest*. On weekends, one of our pastimes was going to open houses in dream neighborhoods. The house we fantasized about had brown shingles, and it was snuggled into its own private forest on the top of a small hill. Through large dormer windows, one could see the Bay on one side, Mount Tamalpais on the other. A large brick fireplace in the living room, another in the palatial master bedroom, and yet a third in the separate living quarters downstairs. That would be for the British nanny.

We would have a sauna, big enough to entertain in—and a hot tub, surrounded by latticework for the ultimate in privacy. Best of all, we would not need a single curtain on any window of the house. We would be nestled into our tree house—no, something even better than that: a tree mansion. This was the perfect place for my happy little family to spend time together. The perfect place to raise a child.

Unfortunately, on one of those weekend excursions, we found it. I say unfortunately because the house was too expensive for us—even though we had always practiced the "anchors away" method of financial growth. "Anchors away" means that you throw your financial commitments around the life-style you want to live, and then pull like crazy until you catch up to it. We had always managed that in the past and it had worked out. We could handle this as well. And so we really worked our way into the house of our dreams.

If my intuitive voice was trying to get through to me, I did my best to ignore it. "Voice to Carol, voice to Carol" was nothing compared to the rush of adrenalin as we made the round to banks, lending companies and real estate offices— finding out with a thrill of delight just how much house we were capable of maneuvering.

We were busy, busy, busy as we got the final papers, rushing against some formidable deadline or other. Signing them. Fanfare. Trumpets.

And then, there was an awful lot of quiet. Too much quiet. Grant was off at school. Dan was at work. And I sat in my new living room. Much too quiet. I heard the voice.

I argued with my little voice. I reassured my little voice. I even squashed my little voice. But it kept saying the same thing over and over to me.

Sell it.

Sell it? The house of my dreams? We had not even unpacked the boxes yet. And I knew, in my heart of hearts, that when I'd signed the papers to the mortgage, I'd signed myself up for fifty-hour weeks at work. Forget the perfect place for my happy little family to spend time together. I would never be home.

I had arrived at the logical, inevitable destination on our road to success—and I was not where I wanted to be.

So what did I do with this clarity of vision? I took up jogging, went for my brown belt, started a class at the junior college and signed Grant up for classes in everything that moved. It took me one full year—count them: three hundred sixty-five days—to get up the nerve to admit to Dan what I had been doing my best to ignore all year. I finally realized that I could go on jogging long blocks and eating cookies—prioritizing and managing my time—until doomsday, and I still would not be happy.

Sometimes, I think about the old days. When I was busy making money, thrilled that I had won this or that honor. I remember how excited I was when I won a Silver Anvil—certain that, by winning my industry's top national honor, I was destined to find complete and total happiness at last. Life was simple then. Hard work and glory. One driven foot ahead of the other, destined for joy and serenity—sooner or later. Young and full of hope that the next raise, the next award, the next child would make the difference for me.

I think about the old days. Sometimes I even wish I could go back. But I can't. Can you?

_____Chapter Seven_____

DRIVE YOURSELF TO HAPPINESS

If you are suddenly suffering from an urge to wash the car, call the office or stick this book in the diaper pail, your little voice probably told you the same thing it told me: "There's no going back."

So ask your little voice a question. "Now what?"

If your voice answers something along the lines of, "Have you figured out what to eat for lunch yet?" or worse, it starts telling you bad jokes, read on.

There's a lot of deferred maintenance going on inside us: unanswered questions, unintegrated opinions, unresolved conflicts and maybe even an undigested wonton or two left over from last night's Chinese take-out. Sitting down and making a list of our priorities only ends up organizing the confusion. Sometimes we think we are getting in touch with some heartfelt conviction leading us to our true higher purpose when, in fact, we have short-circuited on some message leftover from childhood, usually involving guilt.

Is staying up until 4 A.M. tonight to finish this report a joyous expression of self-fulfillment, or just one more feeble attempt to justify your existence on the planet? And for myself, my own special craziness: was selling the house of my dreams an act of courage, destined to deliver my family to the golden land of reduced stress and increased happiness? Or a retreat into the depths of laziness?

After years of hairspray and deodorant, no wonder our innards are gummed up. Aside from those sometimes wonderful, sometimes dreaded occasions when our little voice ambushes us from the rear—we are not skilled in gaining direct access. It's worse than deregulation of the telecommunications industry. You want to direct-dial—only to discover that you don't remember your code, can't figure out how to work the credit card slot and haven't the faintest notion who your long-distance company is.

What it takes—in your phone calls and in your life—is information, skills, practice and action. If you are motivated, you can learn how to connect to who- or whatever is waiting for you on the other end of the line. The more you practice, the easier it will be. In fact, I predict that, before the turn of the century, I will be as comfortable dialing digital codes as I am snapping asparagus tips off with my teeth. With apologies to Ma Bell, I am relatively certain that gaining access to my inner wisdom is likely to occur even sooner.

Willing to give it a try?

Let's start in the slow lane, gathering information before the start of the trip.

_____ *Value Map* _____

Your ideas about yourself are based, in part, on your values. There are certain unshakable principles upon which you base your actions. By grading yourself from one (not important) to five (very important), you will begin to map your own personal value system.

Respect for Your Fellow Human Beings	1	2	3	4	5
Compassion for Others	1	2	3	4	5
Honesty	1	2	3	4	5
Giving with Love	1	2	3	4	5
Patience	1	2	3	4	5
Maturity	1	2	3	4	5

Good. This list is just for starters. You've indicated how important some of these basic human values are to you. You're sure about it. In fact, you'd stake your life on it.

Okay. Let's take these values for a test drive.

Literally. Your car is the perfect laboratory for observation and experimentation for superwomen circa mid-1980s. We spend a lot of time behind the wheel. We drive to and from work. We drive to and from schools, classes and clubs. We drive to appointments and we drive to dates. Most of all, we drive ourselves crazy. Since we are driven, why not drive ourselves someplace we'd really like to be going? Why not drive ourselves to happiness?

For many of us, our time on the road is one of the few occasions when we are all alone. We have time to think, to listen to our very own choice of music and to hiccup without embarrassment. It is also a time when we can do things like practice Kegels. Kegels, for the uninitiated, have to do with strengthening the more private parts of your anatomy in preparation for natural childbirth. The inspiration for this chapter, in fact, comes from the instructor who urged us to practice our Kegels "at every stoplight."

If we could practice Kegels, I realized, we could practice anything. Like Pavlov's dogs, I took the red lights to be signals for all kinds of things. After Kegels, I moved to flossing. When I went through a period of manicures, I'd check my fingernails for chips.

So let's begin our test drive at the next stop sign.

_____*Experiment Number Four*_____

Setup

Before you can make changes in your life, you have to be willing to tell the truth about where you stand. You believe, for instance, that your actions are consistent with your values. As in any good experiment, we begin with simple observation.

The Experiment

The next time you are driving alone in your car, tune in to the incessant chatter going on inside. No, not the drive-time deejay on your car radio. Turn that off. I mean the yakety-yak in your brain.

Now, at the next stop sign, begin to observe your behavior. Not only what you are thinking, but what you are doing. This may be painful, but stick with it. If you feel like you may be lapsing into unconsciousness—if large segments of road and time disappear—don't worry. This is probably your normal state. At every stoplight or stop sign, bring yourself back to your observations.

Analysis

Following are four sample dialog/action scenarios. Pick the one that most closely approximates your own observations.

Dialog/Action Scenario A

Peace, love, happiness. Peace, peas, please! Pass the peas please! Eat them mashed into potatoes. Yeah. Aren't kids great. Happiness is . . . that car in front of me is going too slow. Oh my God, it's going slower. I think I'm going to die if it goes any slooooower. Kids, children, have you hugged your children today? Joanne's such a good friend. I sure do love . . . *I can't stand it!* Get off the road, road hog! HONK, HONK, HONK! Learn to drive, and trash that car while you're at it. I will zonk you with my super zonk-ray eyes. *Kill! Kill!* Thank God. It pulled off. People like that should have their licenses taken away, they should be put in jail. He's an animal! A criminal! A . . . friend of mine? Oh my God, that was Joanne that I just forced off the road.

Dialog/Action Scenario B

This is dumb. Listen to my brain chatter? There's no brain chatter. Nothing going on with me. Absolutely nothing. God, maybe there's something wrong with me. I'm not getting a single thing. Why doesn't my brain function the way she says it will? Maybe I'm doing nothing. That's it. I must already know how to think nothing. Hey, that's terrific. This is pretty easy. I'm getting the hang of it now and . . . whoops. Forgot to stop at the stop sign. What do you mean, waving that finger at me? Yeah? You're one, too, you turkey breeder. Hah-hah! Bet I'd have gotten two points for him. Three, he's so fat. Now, where was I. Oh yeah. It is easy to think nothing. So where's the little voice she promised me? I just don't understand where the little voice is. Here I am thinking nothing, and *no little voice*. It's a rip-off, I tell you. *A rip-off!*

Dialog/Action Scenario C

Speed limit 35. Hah, that's certainly not for me. That's for the town folk, tootling back and forth to the grocery store. I'm another case altogether. I've got important things to do, people to be. Don't you know—you, trying to beat me at the intersection. I know it's your turn—according to the letter of the law. But my car is bigger, shinier, and I am—don't you know—in a bigger hurry to get to more important places than you could ever dream about. On the move. Moving right along. That's right . . . make way for me, part the seas, clear my lane, flash those red . . . uh-oh. Those red lights? That wouldn't be. No. He's going to pass me by. I didn't do anything. What would he want with little me? Oh my God, it *is* me he wants. How dare he! It's not fair! He's picking on me! Just who does he think he is? God, I'm a loser.

Dialog/Action Scenario D

To interpret your findings, turn back to your value map. If your own self-observations most closely approximated Dialog/Action Scenario A, B or C, look to see if you chose all or mostly ones. If you did, congratulations. Your observations support your own willingness to tell the truth about how you have integrated your personal value system into your life. There are congruency and integrity. You are now ready to begin a more advanced practice. Go directly to Experiment Number Five.

If, however, you graded yourself with twos or higher, you're out of touch with reality. You've got a choice here. You can either rescore your value map more honestly, or you can try the experiment again. In fact, you can repeat the experiment daily—twice daily. How about every time you drive your car? When, at last, your thoughts and behavior match your stated values, then you will start to have the quality of life you want.

And what, by the way, if you chose Dialog/Action Scenario D? You are either enlightened, or dead. In any case, you would most probably not be reading this book. So don't bother doing the next experiment.

_____*Experiment Number Five*_____

Setup

In case you chose to keep your value system intact, you will probably be needing some skill development. After being willing to tell the truth, this is the easy part. All you need to do is follow the step-by-step directions of this experiment. Everything I am going to ask you to do is legal and safe. It is also completely unnatural. Stay with it, and good luck.

The Experiment

Take as long as you need to master each of these steps. Try to make it less than one lifetime.

Step One. Drive one mile per hour under the speed limit.

Step Two. Drive one mile per hour under the speed limit without feeling the need to scream. If this is too rapid a progression, merely stop screaming first and work on your feelings as your skill level advances.

Step Three. Be courteous at intersections. Let whoever has the legal right to go first do so.

Step Four. If there is a question about who has the legal right, let the other person have the benefit of the doubt.

Step Five. Smile and wave.

Step Six. Even if the son-of-a-gun was clearly there after you and had absolutely no legal leg whatsoever to stand on.

Analysis

You didn't think you could do that, did you? Smile and wave! How does it feel, to give up rushing against the speed limit—even if only for the duration of the experiment? Nobody's keeping score, you know. You don't get raises or awards for it. You won't even get any flashing lights—not even red ones. All there is is you and that inner satisfaction. A warm glow. That spot—the one that feels good when you reach beyond your programming—that's where the little voice lives.

Driving a car is just like living your life. You can test the limits, speeding down the freeways of your days—resentful and angry at the policeman on patrol. Or you can actually do something about it. Like slow down. You can jam your activities together to justify your fretting about falling behind, or you can free your thoughts for creative purpose. You can rant and rave when you're stuck in traffic, bemoaning the wasted time. Or you can look at the time as an opportunity to observe yourself. Time to take inventory of your thoughts, your values and your behavior. When you observe a discrepancy, you make a correction. Simple as that. Like the gas gauge on the instrument panel. If the needle's low, you don't tell it what a jerk it is. How it should have known better. You take it to the self-serve, and fill it up. Observe and correct.

As you begin to relate to yourself differently, your experiences in life change. The external programming starts to short out. Through the crackling of commercials for microwaves and perfumes, you begin to see an increasing number of choices. In experimenting, you realize that you feel so good, you care less and less about what others think. Observe and correct. Then, before you know it, there is a day—a day that will stand out for you as mine did for me—when you see the traffic stopped ahead, and out of the blue comes a voice. You recognize it immediately: a voice like no other. The voice you have disciplined your chattering mind to let through, practiced listening for, waited patiently to hear. And the voice whispers to you, tinged with excitement, a message you never, ever in your lifetime expected to hear.

"Oh boy! A traffic jam."

---Chapter Eight---

GREAT DEPRESSIONS

The trouble with loving traffic jams is that it's not the kind of thing you can fake. Neither are most of the other things I've been writing about in the last couple of chapters.

There's liable to be a stretch of road between the realization that you would like to make some changes, and the commitment to do so. There's also likely to be a road marker or two between the time you do decide to take action and when the results actually start rolling in.

In retrospect, it is easy to recognize this stretch of time as a time of review and renewal. Old decisions are questioned, new possibilities explored, motivations tested. You try out new ways of thinking and acting, as you discover that the way you used to do things no longer works for you. You come up against the limits of your past experiences, setting out on new terrain. A time to honor yourself, your desire to grow, your willingness to let go of the past.

So you know what these times are called?

The space that happens before you know what to do next: *depression*.

The span between commitment and results: *falling apart*.

This is, obviously, a question of perspective. But for many years—and even now, for many of my friends, members and associates—the perspective we hold is one of white-knuckled terror. We hold on tightly to our dress-for-success suits and buttoned-down minds, unwilling to take any detours on the drive for happiness—especially not through the fear-filled place in my mind, waiting just for me: a bottomless black void, populated by bag ladies who once ran successful public relations agencies.

And don't forget the special detour for women who contemplate neglecting to write personal notes on their Christmas cards.

Such a seemingly insignificant omission may be, after all, just the beginning. An unraveling of the complexities we have assembled for ourselves in the name of coping, balancing and juggling. Lives stuck so tightly together that the removal of a single peg will send the whole thing crashing into disarray. A black void just for them: rolling their shopping carts through the wrong side of town, chained to the burden of boxes of half-priced holiday greeting cards. Not a pretty sight.

Against this fate, we will do *anything* to keep it together. Or more accurately, perhaps I should say we do *everything* to keep it together. We function nicely, going about our tasks efficiently, effectively. We win the respect of our friends and family, the praise of coworkers and journalists alike. Nobody seems to notice that we don't appear to be having a whole heck of a lot of fun. We don't laugh very often, protesting all the while that we are happy. The kind of happy that droops down at the corners. Quietly, we thumb through our dreams: there is a great writer, a world traveler, a passionate romantic. But we don't take them out to put them to the test. A single, failed try is not worth one thousand good illusions.

Treading through our days, keeping an even keel through an ocean of low-grade blues. Remembering past triumphs, past breakthroughs—moments frozen in memory. No longer real or alive, lost in time yet tragically, falsely, incorporated in our current self-images. Things aren't great, but they could be worse. The feeling is, whatever you do, don't rock the boat. Don't take risks. Don't declare yourself. Don't let go of the status quo. Technicolor fantasies. Black-and-white lives.

Give me a great depression any day. Great depressions are what great women have. They feel awful at the time, of course, but they carry with them a quality of nobility: the wisdom to recognize the limitations of one's own circumstances, the consequences of one's own choices, the compassion for one's own aspirations—failed or otherwise.

Reading the autobiographies of such women is always inspiring—although you must admit it is easier to have admiration for another's courage in retrospect, particularly when you know they turned out okay.

Golda Meir was one such woman. Her autobiography, *My Life* (G. P. Putnam's Sons, 1975), presents her inspirational journey to Prime Minister of Israel against the background of her conflicting roles as wife and mother.

When Golda was in her early thirties, she was offered a job as secretary of the Women's Labor Council.

> On the way back to Jerusalem I made up my mind. It wasn't an easy decision to take. I knew that if I took the job, it would involve considerable traveling. . . . But, hardest and most serious of all, I had to face up to the fact that going back to work would spell the end to my attempts to devote myself entirely to the family. . . . Taking on a full-time job, under

the circumstances, meant reconciling myself to this, and the thought frightened me. On the other hand, I told myself that perhaps if I were happier and more fulfilled, it would be better for everyone—for Morris, for the children and for me.

It didn't quite work out that way, of course. Nothing ever works out exactly as one expects it to. But I can't honestly say that I have ever regretted that decision or that in retrospect I think I was wrong to have made it. . . .

The tragedy was not that Morris didn't understand me, but, on the contrary, that he understood me only too well and felt that he couldn't make me over or change me. I had to be what I was, and what I was made it impossible for him to have the sort of wife he wanted and needed. So he didn't discourage me from going back to work, although he knew what it really meant.

If you, too, are willing to break free from old decisions into the Technicolor world of your own declaration, whatever it may be, there is only one way I can think of that does not involve falling into the void somewhere along the way. That is to climb down into it. Grab your flashlight and start exploring. Questioning the meaning of life? Your higher purpose? Feeling helpless! The glue isn't holding, go deeper. Go to the one place where change is most likely to happen. The place that holds the greatest promise of new options, new ways of thinking. Hang out for a while in the place where it is easiest to let go of old ways of acting that have not, cannot and will not take you where you want to go.

Hopelessness.

I know when I am hopeless because my right eye starts twitching. I develop this overwhelming urge to put on the part of the dress that hasn't been torn into washrags yet. I also cry a lot. A whole lot of crying. Hidden behind the dirty clothes bin in the closet with the lights off.

We are talking high drama here. Even writing this gets me twitching. There is heavy emotion mixed into this stew. Some exceedingly unpleasant memories, as well as some currently brewing, thoroughly unwelcome realizations that I will probably—Superwomen's Anonymous membership in good standing and all—do everything in my power to avoid, for a while.

As a casual observer, you might very well look at my life and say, "How wonderful—Carol's in that space that happens just before she knows what to do next."

Oh, yeah? Easy for you to say. When I'm in that so-called space you now think of as "review and renewal," I am in fact hopelessly depressed. Not only that, my life is rapidly falling to pieces.

The one critical difference for me now is statistical. When you have made as many changes as I have in my life over the past couple of years, you've explored a lot of voids. I've shined an awful lot of flashlights in an awful lot of dark corners. Not a single one housed a bag lady. Not even a shopping cart. After I thrash around for a while, sooner or later—one hundred percent of the time—I emerge like some mythological golden-winged phoenix, having successfully navigated that patch of road between realization and commitment, or commitment and results. I've seen myself go through the wringer enough times now to know that I neither fade nor shrink. In fact, I come out new and improved. So, when I feel the glue giving way, I surrender. The faster I get to hopelessness, the faster I'm going to move to the other side. So I go.

When I seriously embarked on making changes in my life, I was already coping quite nicely, thank you. But not enough that I was looking forward to signing my life away to a never-ending treadmill of fifty-hour weeks. For one year, I kept mum about my desire to sell the house. A prisoner of the house, our life-style, the size of the business and of my lost and lonely dreams and ambitions. And you know what the newspapers called me? In full-color, full-page articles, yet? A role model. Superwoman.

When I finally got up the nerve to tell Dan I wanted us to

put the house up for sale, a year had passed. A year of my life gone. If I had known the full ramifications of listing our house for sale, I don't honestly know if I would have had the courage to move forward. They were awesome.

Not the sadness for the loss of material possessions I'd expected to feel . . . the bay views, the three fireplaces. Something far more painful: the first breezes of freedom. An open window, shedding light on old decisions that could now be re-examined. For it soon became obvious that, if we lessened our financial obligations, we would re-introduce choice into our lives. And choice included running the business the way I wanted.

The business was successful. Our salaries were secure. Our reputation firm. Our clients satisfied. And it was all wrong. Somehow, in pursuit of size and status, I had become a manager of people, instead of a practitioner of my first love: public relations. We had grown so large, I did not know my junior executives' last names.

I longed to return to a small, personal company—the kind of hands-on teamwork that had earmarked the early years of my company. The kind of office where employees and bosses respected and enjoyed each other. The kind of place that cared about quality of work and quality of relationships.

I knew what I wanted, but I had no idea how to get there. I was hopeless. The situation was, in fact, hopeless. And out of that realization came a very freeing thought. If the situation was truly without hope, then I could, in fact, stop trying to save it. I could, indeed I had to, try something different.

All of a sudden, clarity flooded into me: the light of truth shined on every corner of my creation. The changes I needed to make were massive. Changes in structure, in personnel, in size. But somewhere, somehow, I found the courage—at long last—to act. I had, in fact, moved beyond choice to a place that has even more power. No choice.

In the midst of pain, I could not yet know that, one year

later, I would find myself surrounded by a staff that shares both the dream and the reality of what business can be at its very best. While we are smaller in size by nearly half, our profits are up.

Best of all, for me, I was able to cut my time back from fifty- and sixty-hour weeks down to twenty or thirty. And the time I'm not at work, I'm not fretting about problems, working overtime trying to make pieces and people fit who would be better off elsewhere. No longer is my life one endless cycle of preparing for work, then recovering from it. As I have shined my flashlight on what were once the issues of my life, one by one, I have done what I needed to do to reclaim them. Our house and our business. But also my relationship to my children, my husband, my parents and friends. And most of all: my relationship to my self.

_____Chapter Nine_____

THE OTHER SIDE

So, am I happy? Imagine this scene. You are sitting in a rowboat, bobbing in the middle of San Francisco Bay. One of your favorite writers, Erma Bombeck, has flown all the way from Arizona to meet you. In a nearby boat is a crew from *Good Morning America*, waiting to take your message to millions of viewers. The sun is playing on the waves, seals are cavorting in your wake. And Erma is asking the question, "Are you happy?"

What do you think the answer is?

I never did tell Erma, sitting there smugly, enjoying the heck out of the moment. But I will tell you.

Sometimes.

Glimpses, moments, an occasional stretch. More and more often now.

My altered state of consciousness.

Happiness.

What I experience the rest of the time, however, is no booby prize. Most of the time I feel real.

Take this morning, for instance. This morning, as I got ready to take a sunrise paddle around the Bay, I felt real. Real cranky, that is.

Wednesdays and Saturdays are my mornings to get up without a care in the world, throw my sweats on and hit the oars. This particular Wednesday, however, Dan—whose co-operation is critical in this maneuver, given the fact that there are two children to dress, feed and deliver to various schools, with appropriate homework, show-and-tell items, bottles and diapers, not to mention a quarter for juice-bar day—is asking for help. Seems that he has booked an early morning meeting that could not be helped and, while he can manage most of it, could I at least change the baby's diaper? Jody, who has not yet mastered the English language, proceeds to add insult to injury by calling me Daddy over and over again. I haven't even left yet, and already she has forgotten my name. Grant is, meanwhile, reminding me that I promised I would wash his jeans. Where are they? Do I dare tell him they are still in the bottom of the shower, covered with the same mud he brought home from school yesterday? I pray I can slip out of the house before he discovers that he is destined to wear dressy pants to school today.

As I slink back upstairs from his room, Jody under my arm, hoping to deliver her to Dan's lap and out the door before the explosion in Grant's room, Dan says, "We're out of milk."

And you have the nerve to ask me if I am happy? Happy? Grant is downstairs tearing through his dresser looking for his jeans, and I am upstairs throwing a fit, because *this is my day, darn it!* And not only is this my regular day to go rowing without a care in the world, but this day—this day during which Dan has the audacity to ask me to change a diaper and to inform me that we are out of milk, is the very day, *the very day* that I am to write the chapter for my book on what it feels like to be happy!

The irony doesn't escape Dan and, as empathetic as he'd like to be, he can't help but laugh. It *is* funny, when you think about it, but who wants to think? It's too much fun to pout to give in to a laugh. At least not just yet. So I slam a door or two, do what I have to, and finally get on to the rowing.

This is my day, and this is my rowboat. But for some reason, the oars feel like they weigh ten thousand pounds. The tide is up, and the water is freezing. I roll my pants up as high as they go, but they still get wet. I nearly tip the scull over when I get in, and the oar splashes salt water in my eye, but I manage to push off. Muttering and sputtering as I go, the water is pushing my oars in the wrong direction. I can't believe it. I have been in this little boat a hundred times, and never have I felt such resistance. Push, push. I'm exhausted, and the boat feels further down the Bay than when I started. I give up. Pull the oars in and drift. Pulling the driving exercise—Exercise Number Four—out of the hat, I watch my thoughts. It's not a car, but let's give it a whirl. *Oooh. Not good.* Lots of poor me, lots of nobody understands me. The boat is rolling gently, and despite myself I'm kind of getting into the little bounces and jiggles. Then I look up. I've been so busy pushing oars that I've forgotten that I am sitting on a huge bay, full of shimmering water. Clouds, like a puffy staircase, ripple the pink horizon. And then, I realize that the water has turned me around. There is a current, and suddenly, instead of fighting it, I am floating with it. I put my oars in the water, and I am flying! The pink sun hits the water and my oars dip in, stirring it in an explosion of pinks, yellows and golds.

The reflections of the birds overhead scatter like a handful of gems as I streak through the ocean of molten gold. Light and free and . . .

Yes: *Happy.*

I have learned along the way that there is nothing I can do to be happy. Oh, I can put myself into situations where happiness is more likely to occur. Like in a rowboat. But I have brought too many uninvited passengers along to even the most wondrous occasion—passengers like jealousy, fear, self-conscious worries—to believe that I can arrange to have a serene mind make a command appearance. When I am bothered, the best I can do is remember to observe my thoughts and my behavior, correct them as best I am able to and, hopefully, bring a little humor to it. Then wait.

Happiness finds me. Like a little bird, it comes to me, usually when I am looking the other way.

When I become aware that the sensation I am feeling is happiness, I recognize that I have been feeling that way for a while without making any particular note of it. The discovery is a pleasant surprise—like coming home to find fresh flowers with a little note attached. No special occasion.

So here I am, paddling around the Bay, splashing up pure gold and diamonds with each pull of the oar. Perfectly at peace—when all of a sudden I start getting ideas. My mind is ablaze with ideas. I know how to write this chapter now. I'll talk about rowing, what I'm feeling out here. I can hardly wait to get back to shore to write all this down. And I am pulling at those oars as fast as I can go, and they have embedded themselves in concrete.

I pull, the boat does not budge. There is a problem. Here is the problem—my hour is not up yet. I have paid my money, rented the boat for a full hour, and I should stay out here in ecstasy for the whole time. Ten minutes to go. Pink waves. Sparkling diamonds. Isn't that nice. Hum. How much longer is there to go now?

And then I realize something about happiness. Like a little bird, you cannot make it come to you—and you cannot hold on to it, either.

When I made the decision to stay in ecstasy for the next

ten minutes, I made the decision by consulting my watch, not myself. My intuitive side was jumping up and down, pulling at the bit to hit the typewriter, but my rational side knew what was better for me. After all, I deserve all the happiness I can get, don't I? I'm now watching the minutes tick away because sitting here—which was so glorious and freeing moments ago—is now "good" for me.

Uh-oh. The same way I realized—déjà vu—that I was happy, I now realize that I am—yuck-yuck-yuck—unhappy. Same water, same oars. Same golden ripples. And I'm starting to think things like, My mother was right about me. And then, thank heavens, I remember to not just have my thoughts—but to observe them. Observe and correct because, while my mother was right about some things, she was definitely not right about others. And for heaven's sake, what am I doing here when what I want to be doing is writing? Laughing at myself, because there's my little bird again—pulling my craft through the slippery gold with ropes of velvet. Lost and found, and lost and found. And so my days go, the little bird coming and going with nary a thought for how corny this image may be. Not only corny, but difficult to move forward into my next thought.

The thought that, if it's been a while since you've felt happiness, you might need to jump-start it to kick in. Somehow, jump-starting a little bird doesn't quite work for me, but I'm hoping I can slip this through by pleading that, as an ex-superwoman, I've given up the idea that I have to do everything perfectly.

So, to jump-start your bird, I've devised Experiment Number Six. Experiment Number Six is a stretch. It requires you to do nice things to yourself for extended periods of time. If you are rusty, it could be more than you can stand. The author, editor and publisher take no responsibility for what may happen to you should you choose to proceed with Experiment Six.

_____*Happiness Experiment Disclaimer*_____

At what age did you last experience unadulterated happiness? Did you seek professional help? Have you ever received disability compensation in conjunction with this situation? Do you release the author, editor and publisher from any consequences that may accrue from whatever happiness you may experience as a result of Experiment Number Six? You may proceed.

_____*Experiment Number Six*_____

Setup

You will need to assemble the following equipment:
1. A hot bath, appropriately scented.
2. Candles and matches.
3. Your favorite music: long-playing.
4. Photo albums featuring pictures of people you have loved, and times you have been happy.
5. A door that locks.
6. Your favorite childhood treat: unlimited quantities thereof.
7. A clean page in a journal or notebook, and a pen that works without splotching.

The Experiment

Combine the various elements in as many different combinations as you can think of for as long as you can stand it.

Analysis

Don't ever analyze happiness. Have it.

Experiment Concluded.

Chapter Ten

BADGES OF HONOR

Congratulations. If you have successfully completed all six experiments thus far, you are on your way to becoming a recovering superwoman. It is time, however, for us to get out of the tub and take ourselves for a spin through our everyday lives.

If you are like most superwomen, your day probably runs something like this.

Alarm! And we step on the adrenalin, getting ourselves and our family up and out, hopefully on time. Careening around the corner to schools, daycare, work. Screeching to a stop, long enough to grab a doughnut for lunch. Revving up again. Speeding through conversations with peers, service people, friends and children. Letting 'er rip through the grocery store to pick up milk and eggs. Holding tight around the curves to exercise class. Pushing it to the floor for one last surge back home: dinner, kids to bed, shake hands with our mates and crash.

We may dream of wide open spaces, fields of wildflowers, faint memories of relaxation and friendship—unencumbered by the ringing of the insistent electronic beep on our designer jogger's watch. Wondering why we are racing so hard and so fast, and not getting where we want to be going. Adventure, creativity, love, self-fulfillment . . . where are they? The scenery is rushing by so fast, we do not even notice that we are not on a road. We are on a track. A circular track. The Superwoman's Le Mans. And this track begins and ends in stress and struggle. No matter how fast and far we drive, we will find nary a wildflower, because there are no flowers at all on this track.

There is an exit, however: a road that leads to open country. Going as fast as we are, it's a blur. To find it, we will need to slow down. It's time for Experiment Number Seven.

_____Experiment Number Seven_____

Setup

Laboratory conditions mandatory. Antiseptic spaces. Locked diaries. Sterilized pens. It is time to take the specimens we have been talking about for nine chapters down off the shelf. Tweezers please. Open the lids. Sorry about the formaldehyde. Now, carefully, lift them out. One at a time. Options. Alternatives. Choices. This is not an experiment for the fainthearted. Shall we begin?

The Experiment

Step One. Rerun the first hour of a typical day of yours in slow motion. Write down the major elements in list fashion:

one item per line. On the first line, put the time you get up. Next line: did you awaken to an alarm? The baby crying? Third line: what kind of bed are you in? And so on through your hour. Who's there with you? What do you do first? Read? Dash downstairs for coffee? Keep going all the way through the hour. Your list should be getting fairly lengthy now.

Step Two. Put a question mark after each item.

Step Three. Forget that this is your life. You are a scientist, and this is your laboratory. After each item, list three dream alternatives. You woke up on a Simmons Beautyrest. One option would be to wake up on a water bed. A second would be a futon. A third would be the floor of a tree house. This is an exercise in creativity. Don't judge or evaluate your options. Have fun with this—take risks with this. What time did you wake up? 7 A.M. and you always wake up at 7 A.M., so there is no possible alternative? Ask yourself why. Because if you get up any earlier, you're tired? What if you went to bed earlier? Get up any later and you'd be late? Could you change the time you go to work? Now nudge your husband awake—if that's on your list. Here's an alternative: you could let him sleep. You could also have him not be there at all.

Don't edit your creativity. Just because you have a thought does not mean you have to do anything about it. This experiment will soon be over, and with it any of the options you let out of their jars. Use this time to expand your creative thinking. How original can you get? At eight every morning you have a cup of tea. At 8 A.M. tomorrow, could you leave for the airport for a quick trip to Paris? Why not? We aren't considering consequences here. Only possibilities. Isn't it fun to give yourself permission to daydream? Why did you put that suit on? Why not a belly dancer costume? Come on. Keep going.

Step Four. Underline the item or option on each line of your list that holds the most appeal for you. You've now created your first dream hour. Don't worry about how or even whether you are going to do this—or any of the other dream hours you now know how to invent. There should be a dozen or so more hours to play with on every one of your days. Designer hours. Created, produced, directed by and starring you and your fantasies.

Analysis

Was this a fun and easy experiment for you? Were you bursting with creative ideas you can hardly wait to try out? Or was it difficult for you to think of alternatives? Did you find yourself censoring some possibilities too threatening to even consider? Were you using hieroglyphic codes, lest somebody should find your list? Worrying about what they would think? Were you editing your choices based on practical considerations? Figuring dollars on your mental calculator? Oh no, on your real calculator? Or how about this: crossing off this one because you might not be good enough; this one, because you might fail? How much of your real day made it to your list? How much of it made it on out of choice . . . and how much out of fear of change? Now we come to the tricky part. Here's where we find out if you are truly a recovering superwoman yet. Just how willing are you to actually make changes in the way you experience your life?

_____*Quality of Life Litmus Test*_____

If You Are Ready to Experience the Quality of Your Life Differently, What Must You Do:

1. Change or quit your job.
2. Leave your husband.

3. Move to a less expensive house.
4. Buy a water bed.
5. ——.

Are you still breathing? Good. Now I will tell you the correct answer. The answer is: Number Five. I told you this would be tricky.

The process of opening yourself up to an expanded number of possibilities is best followed by—right!—doing nothing.

Once again, the way to experience the quality of your life differently is to stop the kind of thinking that got us into trouble in the first place: trying to find happiness by doing things. You cannot decide to change the quality of your life using your rational mind—the same one that makes lists. What your rational mind can do is take the pressure off the gas—make the conscious decision to slow down. When the landmarks in your life come into focus, it will be easier for you to find the way. Perhaps you've already got a gut level intuition about something you want to or feel you have to change right now. Perhaps opening the space through the creative thinking of this exercise allowed some buried truth to surface for you. Let it be, for a while. It won't go away. In fact, as you stay with it for a bit, your certainty that you must act on it will grow. With it, as your commitment to act increases, so will your self-esteem. You have power, you have the ability to act, to make changes. You need not be a victim of old decisions. You may not like going through what you need to face up to in order to change—taking risks. But as your desire to have what you want for yourself becomes greater than your desire to preserve the status quo, the changes will come to your life naturally. Notice, I did not say without pain. We are talking here about making the move from superwoman to great woman. There are no shortcuts, no easy roads that circumvent the tough spots—the need to make hard choices, to stand up for yourself, to take risks and to be willing to experience failure on occasion. What is the source of courage that guides a woman through such rocky terrain? It is trust in yourself, and the belief that as you strip the programming away, what you will uncover is someone destined to evolve toward happiness.

There are lots of philosophers and psychologists who would support this belief. People inspired by the likes of Carl Jung and Abraham Maslow; people like Carol Augustus and Stewart Emery, great thinkers who maintain that each of us has the potential to find happiness—that we have within us the possibility of nurturing healthy spirits—regardless of the circumstances that have affected our behavior. No matter how far into negativity our lives seem to have drifted, we can find our way back to happiness. This is both our privilege and our responsibility: to uncover this potential in ourselves, and to foster it with loving care and encouragement.

Now, take this sensibility for a jaunt through our popular literature. Helen Gurley Brown's *Having It All* (Linden Press, 1982) in a section titled "Don't Be Your Own Best Friend!" quotes author Margaret Halsey from a *Newsweek* editorial. "Inside each of us is a mess of unruly, primitive impulses." Helen writes she "couldn't agree more . . . heavy self-love must be earned."

Against the philosophical backdrop enunciated by Halsey and Brown, no wonder we are afraid to let up for even a moment, lest those unruly primitive impulses turn us into bag ladies, sloths or "just a housewife"—whichever happens to be your worst fear.

We are scared to death that, if we were to adopt the point of view that we are really okay inside, "we may never be motivated to move onward." Are we, in truth, likely to turn into lazy, self-indulgent good-for-nothings? Is there anything in your own personal history that supports that fear? Okay, so you didn't complete your master's. Resent fixing the baby's bottle at three in the morning? Serving TV dinners to your family? These aren't impulses from unruly, primitive places. These are normal, natural inclinations. If you are a superwoman, you need to start with the premise that your life is aimed at generating fifty percent more useful behavior than is healthy for the human organism to try to produce. Fifty percent may not be accurate. For many of us, it's more like seventy-five. I trust myself and I trust you that if we stop driving ourselves so hard, we will still accomplish enough to justify our existence on the planet. In fact, we might even conceivably realize that we are still worthy of love. We might even begin to enjoy our time here on Earth.

Because we have worked so hard and been so good for so long, I have a special treat for us. The Superwomen's Anonymous Handbook Badges.

These badges are like no other you have ever received. They are only for those of us who have successfully completed all seven experiments thus far. Segments of the population who have not suffered from prepeaking superwomanitis or superwoman-role-modelitis do not qualify for them. May you earn and wear these badges with honor. You deserve each and every one.

The Mediocrity Badge

After many years in pursuit of excellence, it is time for you to evolve to the next step. Mastering the art of being selectively average.

This is no easy task. For individuals trained in overachievement, the race is on between learning how to be mediocre at will versus burning out.

No one feels particularly proud of being average. I'm an average cook. I'm a mediocre tennis player. These are not the kind of things that earn the admiration of those around you. Such admissions, however, can be badges of honor. Here are a few reasons why:

1. If you don't allow yourself to be average at some things, you might not allow yourself to do something you'd truly like to do but would not do well. I, for instance, enjoy singing. I am also a mediocre singer. For years, I avoided singing because I couldn't do it excellently. Now, I sing excellently in a mediocre way and am perfectly content.

    My karate instructor said something inspiring about this. Having watched a procession of super-achievers attend a class or two of instruction only to discover that karate is harder than they thought and quit, he now tells beginners, "If it is worth doing, it is worth doing badly."

2. If you don't allow yourself to be average sometimes, you may provide more or better service than is called for. If you consistently provide more than is called for, your value may drop. Your boss or client will raise his or her expectations of you—without necessarily raising your salary. It is easy to get into a slow burn over this. Know, instead, that the time to deliver excellence is when that is what is satisfying to you, when it is called for and/or when it will be rewarded. Establish the criteria for compensation—internal or external—in advance of delivery. If the criteria fall consistently below your desire and ability to deliver, change situations. You are ready to play in a bigger game.

To earn the Mediocrity Badge, you must fulfill the following criteria:

1. Think about something you've always wanted to do that might be difficult for you.

2. Do it.
3. No matter what.
4. Look to your internal satisfaction, acknowledging your process of growth.
5. Even if you are the worst in the class.

_____ *The Unpopularity Badge* _____

You were born to please. If it wasn't mommy and daddy, it was Gloria Steinem and Jane Fonda. Now it's time to confront the big one. The one everybody's been afraid to tell you, lest the entire fabric of your life to date be ripped apart. At the end of life—when the Grim Reaper comes to get you—he does not even begin to resemble Bert Parks. What's more, he does not have a prize for you, even if you rated as Miss Congeniality. While you were busy worrying about not offending others, about being liked, about fitting in, about making life easier for them, they were putting glue in your toothpaste and grabbing the roses for a walk down the runway.

Now, I know that not everybody puts glue in your toothpaste. Hopefully, you have surrounded yourself with people who love you, support you and care about you—even if you don't do everything they tell you to. Friends understand that it is more important for you to have a grip on the truth and to act on it with courage than to please them. When the gods are smiling, their truth and your truth coincide.

When they don't? That's one of those moments when choices, options and alternatives still reek of formaldehyde. You may be tempted to stuff them back in your jars, screw on the lid, and convince yourself that it wasn't what you wanted anyway. Or, you may hold your ground and take the consequences. The bottom line, unfortunately, is that you have only one life to live—you can live your own life, or you can live somebody else's.

For die-hard people-pleasers, the possibility of doing something that may prove unpopular may seem awesome. My suggestion to you: start small. Find out that you can say no, and survive. Start with the cat, if you need to. "No, you may not eat my favorite cashmere sweater." Work up from there. Understand that it may be some time before you confront the big issues. Sneak up on them one step at a time. After the cat, you will have what it takes to earn this badge. To do so, you must fulfill the following criteria:

1. Say no the next time you are asked to do something you don't want to do, don't have to do, and shouldn't do—but would have felt you had to anyway.
2. Do so without apologizing, explaining and without offering fair exchange alternatives you are just as eager not to do.
3. If there's negative fallout, stand your ground.
4. If word gets back to you that you are a certain kind of so-and-so for doing so, laugh.
5. Then forget about it.

The Good-for-Nothing Badge

Superwomen are always good for something. If they aren't out earning money, they are mowing the lawn or saving the whales. If they take a stress reduction class, the point is to get a handle on things so they can go out and accomplish even more.

So, while superwomen are busy earning their keep, justifying their existence and having what it takes to get the job done, all kinds of lovely things happening every day go unnoticed, unappreciated and are basically useless. Things like sunrises and sunsets. If Nature followed the same basic principles as most superwomen, she would have done away with them long ago. Rainbows are not particularly practical, either. They do not fit in the chain of life: the one we hear about when the rare stinkfish is threatened by the developer's bulldozers, and we all rally to save them, because if they go, sooner or later we will all go. If rainbows go— aside from the fact that the laws of physics would need to be reversed and we would probably all be traveling backward through time to a different dimension—we would probably not even notice. Rainbows don't help the economy, iron shirts or serve as food for slightly bigger fish. They just hang around, providing joy and beauty for those of us still awake enough to remember to look up.

Depending on how far gone you are, some of you right now are probably coming up with a solution for this problem. A new organization: Save the Rainbows. Not this time. Instead of saving the rainbows, let's *be* rainbows. Let's be the kind of useless beauty that just hangs around from time to time. A magical presence, there to be enjoyed by any who choose to tune in—but not dependent on that for justification of existence.

I don't have a badge for rainbows, but I do have a badge for the next best thing: a place to start practicing what it would take to have that kind of presence. The Good-for-Nothing Badge. To earn it, you must fulfill the following criteria:

1. Think of something you'd like to do that would be a complete waste of your time.
2. Ask yourself if this activity has any redeeming value whatsoever.
3. If it does, think of something else that does not.
4. Do it.

_____ *The Failure Badge* _____

The only way to minimize the potential for failure is to do
only what you already know you can do. The instant you
contemplate the possibility of trying something new, different or expanded, you come face-to-face with the possibility of failure. Now, if you are like most superwomen,
you are saying the following: You don't mind taking risks—as
long as you know that you will not fail. That's not a risk.
Don't fool yourself. You have just come up with fancier pack-
aging—but all the ribbons and foil in the world won't change
the contents of the package. Risk will. And risk always holds
the potential for failure. Think about times you have tried
something and failed. If your stomach can take it, for instance, think of your first boyfriend. You were probably too
young and green to even realize that you were taking a risk
at the time. You found that out later when he jilted you.
Remember how awful that was? The sun was not going to
shine again. And if it did, you'd go inside and pull the
shades. Life without Ricky or Johnny was not worth living.
Oh yeah? Now think about this. What if you hadn't failed?
You and Johnny are now married twenty or thirty years. His
huge gum bubbles—such a source of pride then—are now a
grave irritation to you.

How about some other losses? Fired from a job? Your
great novel rejected? As time has told its story, what new
opportunities or awareness opened for you as a result of
these disappointments? If select failures in the past can now
be seen in a less threatening light, how about select failures
in the future? What if that business you've been too afraid to
start actually did fail, but out of that came a dream job offer
to head up a division for a former competitor? Since you
can't live your life backward, you must proceed as if anything that risks bring to you—success or failure—is ultimately for the good. Honor yourself for being willing to

fail. To earn your Failure Badge, fulfill the following criteria:

1. Go ahead and do something you have really wanted to do, but were afraid to.
2. Succeed or fail.

If you don't want to earn these badges— if you don't want to navigate the tough terrain wherein may lie personal satisfaction for even, yes, superwomen, then please—for all our sakes—at least have the good grace to stop complaining about your lot in life, and let's get on with it.

Chapter Eleven

DOWNWARD MOBILITY

As a generation, the post–World War II boom babies have been through a lot over the past several decades. In the sixties, we believed that freedom meant that we had limitless options and potential. We began an exploration that led us to such altered states of consciousness as bean sprouts and self-induced poverty. In those halcyon years, we wore our "essence" on our sleeves.

In the seventies, we narrowed down our options—trading in flower-bedecked VW vans for sporty little cars with great mileage. Nevertheless, we believed we were still doing our thing. But now, it was the responsibility of other people to "get" who we really were.

In the eighties, we have eliminated virtually all the options and we are less concerned about the essence of ourselves than with that of whatever happens to be in our Cuisinart at the time.

I, for one, have no desire to turn the clock back. I believe that most of the options I eliminated deserved to be dumped. I never did care much for sprouts. But I'm getting tired of my espresso machine as well. When French cuisine turned nouvelle, I stopped in awe, struck by the beauty of my first kiwi. The weirder the fruit, the more quality in my life. I measured happiness by how much a pound at the checkout stand. I especially liked the grocery stores that individually wrapped each mushroom in tissue paper. They didn't charge by the pound, but by the karat.

I was in ecstasy the first time I tasted a bouquet of Japanese mushrooms: the kind that come a dozen to a single stem, like bursting white heads of pins. Rolling the new flavors around with my tongue. Guided by individuals with knowledge superior to mine through the joy of liberating the meat from a mesquite-grilled soft-shelled crab. But, alas, even kiwi loses its romance the fourth or seventh or tenth time. The restaurant reviewers agree, harkening back to home-style country cooking as this year's novelty item—while praying for something new and wonderful, like snail's eggs—honest to God—to entice our tongues back to attention.

Somewhere along the line, even before the snail's eggs, I lost interest. It came around the time my Diner's card exceeded my monthly income.

I knew I was in trouble when my hankering for kiwi deserted me. Sprouts went with the sixties, fondue with the seventies and now kiwi. I questioned the meaning of life.

I had, in my estimation, now succeeded in eliminating the last acceptable external option for me. Already gone was the desire for a bigger and better car. What could you possibly hope for when you already have a Porsche 911 SC Targa? We'd been to Europe. We had our own business. My wardrobe read like a Fifth Avenue directory.

I thought of dropping out. I tried to enroll Dan in the

concept. We'd cash out, buy a mobile home on the edge of a national park, and forage for nuts and berries. I'm big on creative thinking. I'm not, however, big on nuts and berries. Happily, Dan dug in his heels. In time, the panic mellowed. But life without options is no fun.

I was too far along, disengaged from defining myself on the basis of what I had or did to continue marching in step with the yuppies. But I could not see growing our hair back and moving to the country either. I couldn't even get a potato to sprout for Grant's class project, let alone grow my own food. There was no road map or markers for myself as it became increasingly clear that, if I was to move forward, I was going to have to make up the route.

Luckily, my desire to cut back from my work—to take the time to re-inject some vitality into my life—had financial implications. I say luckily, because our incipient battle with budgeting led us into a rich underground of financial innovators. People like financial advisor Roger Pritchard, budgeting whiz Robert Ortalda and prosperity psychologist Dr. Ruth Ross. I studied their ideas, added a few twists of my own and voilà . . .

_____*Experiment Number Eight*_____

Setup

What does prosperity mean to you? What would it take for you to have the experience that you are a prosperous person? To do this experiment, you will need a shiny metal object. A magic lantern will do. If you don't have one on hand, rub your Italian espresso maker.

The Experiment:

Step One. Imagine that the magic genie of prosperity has just popped out of your Italian espresso machine. He is going to grant you every dream you've ever had related to prosperity. Make a list of what the genie is granting you. Ask yourself: What can you summon the genie for that will really, truly, once and for all make you happy?

Step Two. If you got all that, would you be happy then? If not, keep going. Okay. How about now? When your list is complete, go to *Step Three*.

Step Three. You know darn well there's no such thing as a magic genie. So now, add up the total costs of all the items on your dream list. Divide it by your and/or your husband's hourly wage.

Step Four. You realize now that, to get the things that will really make you, once and for all, truly happy, you will have to work that many hours, that much harder and longer. You'd better add a few more items to your dream list to make the extra effort worth your while.

Step Five. Now, add up the total costs of all the items you've added to your dream list. Divide it by your wages.

Step Six. You're going to have to work harder for all that? You'd better add a few more perks to make it worth your while.

Step Seven. And so on, ad nauseam.

Analysis:

The only way off of this Möbius strip is to wish for what you really want in the first place rather than for what you believe might create the experience of what you really want. I am thinking here of qualities like love, happiness, peace. Did they even make it to your list? Remember, I didn't say the genie could only create material goods. Did you read it that way? Or are you starting to see the exit ramp off the Superwoman's Le Mans?

Before my studies, I would have defined prosperity as the experience of happiness created by the accumulation of material resources. An alternative point of view on prosperity, the one that I have come to adopt as my own, is that it is simply the experience of having enough.

To comprehend the enormous implications of this thought, we need to flip it upside down for a moment. In the pursuit of material wealth as a key to the creation of happiness and satisfaction, the great majority of us have stumbled onto a fundamental flaw in the system. As I learned in the workshop Thin Within, you can't have enough of what you don't want. Think of celery for a moment. How many diets have you been on where by the second day—or second hour, depending on how far gone you are—you are craving a Hostess Ho Ho. You look at your list of acceptable foods, and pick the one item that your diet allows in unlimited quantities. Usually celery. So, you go to the grocery store and buy a cart full of stalks. Take them home, wash them, groom them and devour them. Stalk after stalk after stalk. Your tummy is stuffed, your jaw is aching. And, having ravaged them down to the leaves, you lean back waiting for satisfaction to arrive. Something comes. That's for sure. But it's not satisfaction. What comes is, you got it, a craving for Ho Hos. So now, you've already eaten the equivalent of Farmer John's entire winter crop of celery—the commodities market is reeling with the impact—and you finally figure out that nothing, nothing in the world other than a Hostess Ho Ho is going to make you happy. Perhaps you make it through another hour or two, but then the dam breaks. In a frenzy, you careen through the streets to the market—you eat the Ho Hos even as you stand in the checkout line—bits of brightly colored paper marking your path. So now, not only have you eaten 1000 calories of celery (nearly 150 stalks at 7 calories apiece), but you have also eaten what you were craving in the first place: the Ho Ho.

Now, think how hard you and/or your husband work to support your past obligations and future plans. Paying for all the things—like celery—that you hoped would satisfy your cravings. Things like computers, VCRs, BMWs and dream homes. In retrospect, would you have liked to have more time for yourselves, for your family? Time for reading, for creating, for playing, for—dare I even say it—hanging out? Now it's time to put this experiment to use. Look around your house and your life at all the things you have accumulated. Remember how happy you felt when you opened the box, made the purchase, plugged that particular appliance in for the first time? How long did the experience last? Have you already purchased a superior version—bigger, better or more? Now ask yourself how much of your house you actually use? The living room that nobody ever goes to; the spare bedroom that has been turned into a storage area?

These are the kinds of questions Dan and I began asking ourselves as our desire to claim creative, nurturing time for ourselves individually, as a couple and as a family, became greater than our desire to accumulate more wealth.

We, as most of our generation, had gotten trapped in the idea that prosperity meant that we not only deserved, but that we had the historical imperative to create an even better life-style than our parents ever achieved. After all, we were the generation that had all the advantages.

So there we were, Dan, Grant, Jody and I, living in our dream house—working round the clock to support the live-in's quarters that were unoccupied due to the fact that, four live-in's later, we realized we didn't like strangers in the house. Supporting the espresso maker and hot tub that had been cause for celebration early on, but eventually took the fun out of special visits to coffee houses and spas. Supporting the red leather seats of the car that were now stained with spilled milk from the baby's bottle.

We, like many of our generation, were living our lives upside down. Rather than ask ourselves how we wanted to spend our time—what we really needed to support the quality of our lives, we were accumulating things in the illusion that they could create quality. Mistakenly, we felt that if we hadn't found it yet, it was just that we hadn't tried enough combinations in a trial-and-error process that never seemed to create the illusion of *enough* for more than a day or two. We threw out our salary aspirations like nets to the herrings, hoping that they would rake in enough for happiness. We guessed we'd need fifty thousand, or one hundred thousand or half a million to finally have enough. Raises came—but the initial relief was soon engulfed by new needs, new obligations.

When I decided to pull back from work, we knew we would have to come to terms with the economic implications. For over a year, Dan chose to make up the difference. He would keep our house and income by working longer and harder: he wound up giving more than one pint of blood, sweat and tears at the office.

Eventually, working part-time and exploring other possibilities the rest of the time, I became happier and lighter: excited about my new journal class, about the discovery of secret poetry that had been hidden for several decades in my heart, of new friendships and adventures. Dan, on the other hand, was burning out.

What was working for me in our new arrangement, and working well, was not working for Dan.

We first went for financial planning to find new ways to cope: to juggle, manage and organize our investments and our debts. Calling on an old friend in the business, I should have known better. He did, after all, work out of Berkeley. What he suggested to us was not a better place to shelter our income, but rather, a reduction in our life-style.

Downward mobility.

I was shocked, until I heard the entire concept. Downward mobility did not have anything to do with dropping out. It had to do with choosing what you want in your life with care and selectivity. Quality as opposed to quantity; the elegance of simplicity—a concept the Japanese call *shibumi*.

While we'd brought our calculator along, our friend gave us a far more challenging assignment than figuring bank balances. He asked us to find three individuals or couples who had willingly chosen to reduce their life-style. As I opened my eyes, I realized they were nearer to me than I thought, quietly, happily opting for downward mobility out of choice—as opposed to those who got there through default. The ones who do opt for this simple paring down generally don't make a lot of noise. They generally don't write books or go on television talk shows, either. (I suspect that, had I had more experience in this blessed state under my belt prior to putting out my little newsletter, I would have kept mum too.)

Eventually, I found them. One was right under my nose. A woman who had left an executive job with a clothing manufacturer to embark on a career change to something that would provide more satisfaction. In the meantime, she was cooking meals part-time for home-delivery, discovering in the process that she was a lot happier puttering around the kitchen part-time and exploring the riches of new adventures with family and friends during the rest of her time. Her car was so old, it could barely stay together for deliveries, let alone make it for a swing around the Superwoman's Le Mans. She did look awfully happy, however.

The second was my karate sensei, a man who left his career as a computer executive to live his life as a samurai— as best one can in this day and age.

The third and fourth were my parents, who had moved out to California from our home in Chicago to retire. Wistfully, I had watched them disengage from their careers, having spent decades curing more tonsillitis and teaching more people to read, respectively, than I could begin to imagine. These two dynamos now had the time I wished I had, to enjoy it with my own children, visit the local museums, travel across town to buy the perfect loaf of bread from that one bakery that really understands rye.

I wanted all that: the time for exploration and adventure, the passion for doing something I truly cared about, the appreciation of simpler things that contain so much beauty.

The thought occurred to me that, if previous generations like my parents' had learned to make ends meet on one paycheck, what if Dan and I also lived on one? Only this time, instead of taking turns supporting each other, we would try teamwork. Together we would create our income. Job sharing: husband and wife.

Where I had once been afraid to touch any single portion of our intricately organized lives—in fear of a massive unraveling—I now dug in with pick and shovel. Dan was at my side, slicing credit cards into shreds, putting everything we didn't particularly care about in the garage for what was to be, eventually, the garage sale of the century. You want it, it's yours! Even the garage. That went, of course, with the house. The one with the view of the Bay, the three fireplaces and the huge mortgage.

Kiwis went. So did convenience foods with high prices and lists of ingredients ending in words with lots of Xs in them. I cleaned out the closets: all the clothes that lay in wait for their moment in the sun. A moment that had come and gone before I'd left the boutique but after I'd signed on the dotted line.

We were clearing the cobwebs out of the darkened corners of our attic, our garage, our closet, our life. Feeling physically, mentally and emotionally lighter as we emptied our house.

Opening up the space, literally, for something new to

happen for us. Something of our own choosing: right for who we were, and who we were becoming. Not things to make us feel better, to make us happier: but to fulfill some basic functions in our life—nourish our bodies, provide us with comfort, or simply and importantly enough, provide us with the experience of beauty. The Porsche stayed. In Dan's opinion, that car is the ultimate expression of the spirit of man on wheels. So did our fine china, our scheduled vacation to Hawaii and some very expensive wine we both enjoy immensely. Grant kept his Voltron, but dispensed with boxes full of Santa's surrender to advertised toys of Saturday morning television past. Jody has not yet figured out that she has been looking adorable all of her life in friends' lovingly shared rompers. I have only been caught on one or two occasions staring longingly at $100 coat/hat/legging sets inspired by Shirley Temple. The frilly dress, she got.

We looked for and found a new home: half the size, mortgage and commute as what we'd thought was the house of our dreams. This house is like a country cottage—down to the white picket fence.

Eventually, with a commitment to this process over time, everything in our life has become precious. We've begun to see that downward mobility is not a matter of doing and having less: it is a matter of doing what you want. We began to apply the principles of prosperity to all aspects of our lives: not just our material possessions. Relationships, jobs, self-fulfillment: we learned that we had ample resources to create the space for what we truly wanted in our lives, but also that what we wanted looked very different from what we had always believed it would.

The ultimate irony of downward mobility is that, by beginning to care about the things we have and do for the right reasons, a newfound vitality was injected. Where producing results through our work was once an effort, we now feel inspired to aim for them. When Dan and I cut our hours at work back from fifty to twenty, we reduced the size of our business to accommodate this fact. We expected to cut our salaries as well. But an amazing thing occurred. As we cut our overhead in half, our profits increased. With time to nurture our creativity, we brought more to our clients than all the hours in the day could ever have provided previously. Our ideas were inspired. Our staff was motivated.

The ultimate irony, of course, is the immense success of Superwomen's Anonymous. All my life, I dreamed of using my talents at communication and promotion to shed some additional light on our planet. But there I was, year after year, working longer, harder and better at the business, looking for a way to do so—while using my skills to shed light, instead, on a new brand of salami. I surrendered finally, giving up my worldly ambitions, enjoying—in their place—the quality of my friendships, my children and my relationship to Dan. I journaled. I rowed. I dreamed. And I decided, one day, to play a joke on my friends. I would take a day to put together an organization for superwomen that would hold no meetings, classes or fund-raisers, and ask them to join.

Now, we're a phenomenon. I am inspired. My spirit is soaring. If this had happened to me as recently as two years ago, I probably would have thought, "Oh boy!" and started to feel that I deserved to look for a more glamorous home. But we had just moved from our more glamorous home.

I like our little country house just fine, thank you.

Try to figure me out, make your best guess, and guess what? Chances are, you will be wrong. At times, I may choose to take off from work. Or I may choose to work even harder. I may spend more time with my family, or less. To the outside world, there may not seem to be much difference from how I was living before. Or it may look very different. In any case, most of the time I feel too alive to care what it does or doesn't look like to anyone else. I am, at last, beginning to live my own life. Not only do I have enough, I *am* enough. And, as we all know, enough is enough.

PART III

Impacting Our Families, Ourselves, Our World

Chapter Twelve

SIMPLE MEN, COMPLICATED WOMEN

By now, you are probably getting the general drift that options like downward mobility, the art of unpopularity and letting things fall apart for a while could possibly have an impact on another segment of the population: namely, our men.

Let's face it, women. We are a handful. As Dan has said to me on more than one occasion, "Has it ever occurred to you that not only are you enough . . . you are too much!"

Poor men. It's been one heck of a decade for them. First, they resisted the notion that the women in the generational pool wanted to compete with them for the plum jobs instead of standing in line to tend their home and hearth.

When men finally figured out that the ambitious women they were meeting were not aberrations, but rather the way of the future, they surrendered.

One way or another, women gained entry into the private clubs, the executive suites and the corner offices. Like undercover agents, we brought a few extra roles along for the ride. The parts of us that have traditionally served as caretakers of the human spirit, for instance. Qualities like compassion and sensitivity that do not necessarily have a direct impact on the economy, but provide a few useful functions around the house or office—like make life worth living, for example. From our relatively new perspective—unencumbered by genetically modified brain circuitry—we realized that the price of success in the working world was dear. Not only for women, but for men, as well.

As we are waking up, beginning to ask such dangerous questions as, "Is this all there is?" we are taking our men with us. They may not be fully aware of this yet, but all those corporate vice presidents—the ones who we know carry yellowed photos of themselves with long hair and beards secretly tucked into the hidden crevices of their Gucci wallets—are looking on with great interest. Remember the sixties—all those dreams? We all vowed we would never sacrifice our values to cop out like the older generation. We moved thousands of miles away to prove just how different we were. Now we are scrambling to live in each other's parents' houses, join their clubs, drive their cars. Like a set of musical chairs, the geography may have changed, but the game is essentially the same.

We toast each other in the finest restaurants, but there is a restlessness there. Men know we are stressed out. They know the pressures we are under. They know the guilt we feel as we let our children, our friendships and our values slide. But they are confused, not knowing what they can do to help. They are already doing far more around the house than any previous generation of men in western history. Despite the fact that they still may expect a Nobel Prize every time they change a diaper, they have been force-marched into a relationship with their children that contains the intoxicating seeds of vulnerability and compassion. Secretly, they are beginning to crave it.

As our men move through the eighties and up the corporate ladder, more and more they will have the power to express their own integrity. From vice president to president, corporation after corporation will have to find the space to accommodate our surfacing values. Just as they learned to reckon with women in the seventies, they will expand to make room for considerations relating to the quality of life in the eighties. This is, perhaps, a Californian's optimism. We are, after all, residents of an environment that more and more offers maternity leaves for men as well as for their wives, provides child care on premises for the employees, four-day work weeks, flexible hours, job-sharing and periodic sabbaticals for executives.

If this sounds good to you, why don't we pitch in together and make it happen?

How?

One step at a time.

And step one is simply this. Realize that you are not the only woman in the world who has it all and feels inadequate. Know that you deserve to have the time and space in your life it takes to nurture close relationships with your children, your friends, your spouse. That you deserve intimacy, creative expression and self-fulfillment, adventure and love and serenity and excitement and a whole array of wonderful things.

Step two is knowing that the men in our lives deserve this, too . . . even your boss, if your boss happens to be a man.

You and your husband might be a little rusty now, but think back to when you first got together. As in the case of Prince Charming and Sleeping Beauty, romance brought with it the promise that now all your dreams could come true. That probably lasted through day two of your honeymoon, when you realized that your newly beloved has the nasty habit of putting his gum under the table.

Chances are that you've spent most of your relationship in various states of repressed resentment. Remember how you felt when you first discovered there is no Santa Claus? Multiply that by 8, place that on the Richter scale, and you will begin to glimpse the disappointment the majority of us feel when we realize that, however great the illusion of romance, when push comes to shove we will have to make it on our own. We think we'd like to be taken care of—but, as our mothers found out, the price is too high. No dream house, no kiwi and no man can provide more than a temporary high—as long as we are looking to external sources for the creation of our happiness.

Clever as we have become at keeping ourselves busy having, doing and being everything we can be, so have superwomenized couples learned to delay the moment of reckoning for as long as possible.

Are you one of these?

—————————— *The Entertainers* ——————————

Couple number one love to have a good time. Their weekends are booked through the early 1990s. When there's a spare moment, you can count on them to think of something wonderful to do. They have each mastered the social graces, providing scintillating conversation and marvelous commentary. They are great at Trivial Pursuit. You wouldn't know this from looking at them—and even they haven't figured it out yet—but they haven't had the opportunity to say a word directly to each other for several years now. And if they play their cards right, they may make it through a few more.

The Sufferers

Couple number two stopped bothering a long time ago. They live in the same house, but then, so do the termites. She is heavily involved in community organizations. He is immersed in work. When they speak to each other it is usually to complain. He thinks she should keep the house tidier. She thinks he should spend more time with the children. Each of them has considered separation but dismissed the thought. After all, when all is said and done, they do have a lot in common. All that suffering.

The Parents

Couple number three are dedicated to the children. They wouldn't think of taking a vacation without them. Family outings are the highlight of each week. Activities center around the school, the scout troop, the soccer league. What with practice after school, jigsaw puzzles and nighttime stories, it's lights out for everybody at 8 P.M., even when the kids are gone.

The Negotiators

For couple number four, every chance encounter is a summit conference. Wheeling and dealing career and household assignments, the balance of power is maintained at all costs. Dinner is the perfect time to handle the budget. Bedtime is a fine time to stabilize chore delegation. The only thing that never seems to make it onto the table is love.

_____*The Lone Ranger*_____

Couple number five are not two people. It's single super-mom, who just thinks she is a couple. She is having, doing and being everything she can—including father and mother—to her children. She is so convinced that she can do it all on her own, she has long ago stopped bothering to ask herself if that's what she really wants.

You have to admire the human animal. When faced with the demise of romantic illusion, do they squawk about like chickens? No, they adapt by mastering ever more sophisticated versions of avoidance.

You really can't expect any more of them. After all, it is a rare individual—male or female—who even begins to understand that happiness is something that must come from within. Even then, that individual is lucky to have an occasional experience—like my precious moments out on the bay in my rowboat—of anything that comes close to pure, unadulterated joy. So now, you try to find two individuals who are on to this. Put them together, and hope that their momentary experiences of joy happen to coincide: you've got a mathematical formula that has an awful lot of zeros in it—as in, one in a million chances of that happening.

When they do come together—and I promise you that they can—what you have is Major Magic.

But in the meantime, while you have patiently let those statistical zeros run their course, what is one to do?

You're not going to like my answer. Not one bit.

The alternative is to be real with your man. If you ever hope to have a relationship with him that is more than an entertaining, productive or manageable way to pass the time, you will have to let yourself be vulnerable.

You will, for instance, start practicing with your very own mate, the skills taught throughout this book: taking risks, sharing feelings, asking for what you want. You may cry together, scream together and eventually love together.

I propose that there is something even greater than Prince Charming awaiting the miracle of our generation. With vulnerability and compassion, there comes the potential for real teamwork. As superwomen, we have proven that we are capable and willing to shoulder an economic burden. Through teamwork, the recovering couple can begin to look at how we can change our personal economy so that we can both begin to fulfill our potential as human beings. Rather than throw the burden of responsibility for career, children and personal values back and forth like a hot potato, the couple can start to pull the oars together.

Only then will we begin our real journey through the riches of a relationship together.

Experiment Number Nine

Setup

We've talked a lot about compassion in this chapter: how it is one of the special qualities women have to bring to the world, both in work environments and their own homes. For our generation of superwomen, I'd have to say that this quality exists more as a potential than as an actualized experience: at least as it relates to the men in our lives. When we tune in to our feelings, we may tap into a vein of anger, frustration and pain. What then? Turn into screaming banshees, rightfully demanding that our husbands do things our way? As we are evolving our own sense of self, do we expect them to pick up the pieces—take care of us while we go and explore our true potential? If we let the resentment of failed fantasies past run us, that is exactly what we will do. If, on the other hand, we forgive our husbands for not being everything we want them to be—and if we forgive ourselves—we have the basis for a mature relationship. And a mature relationship, in turn, is the basis for love. Maturity is not necessarily something that comes with age. For many of us, it will be a lifelong study and practice. What it does mean is simply this: I know and respect myself for who I am in this relationship. I am getting to know you—and respect you as well—in this relationship. That does not mean, however, that this relationship should or ought to take whatever form it has taken in the past. When you are in good communication with your inner wisdom, you will know if you are in a relationship that is, in its current form, nurturing to you. You will know what else is possible for you, and how to get there. The first thing, in any case, is to do this experiment.

Experiment

The next time your mate falls short of your expectations, picture him as a four-year-old. Imagine that, at that tender age, he has neither the skills nor the maturity to have handled the situation any differently. See if you can feel it within you to mentally hug him, tell him that while you are still disappointed, you know he was doing his best. From this perspective, now communicate your feelings out loud to your mate, holding the image clearly in your mind.

Analysis

This is a powerful experiment, since many of the people in our lives—mothers, fathers, employees and even, of course, yourself—have actually not evolved to any substantial degree emotionally since childhood. We all crave to be taken into somebody's arms when we fail. We want somebody to stroke our brow and tell us that, even though we've fallen short of expectations, we are still loved. A mature individual can provide this nurturing for themselves, and reach out to others as well.

Chapter Thirteen

SUPERCHILDREN VERSUS GREAT CHILDREN

Are You Raising a Superchild?
_____*Take This Quiz and Find Out . . .*_____

The number of activities my child has been/is involved with
is more or less than two times his or her age (rounded up):

More	2 points
Less	no points

The party favors at my child's last birthday cost:

Zero to $3 each	no points
$3 to $5	1 point
$5 and up	2 points

My child has one or more of the following chic ailments:

Stomachaches	1 point
Ear infections	1 point
Allergies to milk, cats or mold	1 point
Allergies, nonspecific	2 points

My child goes to:

A public school	no points
The public school	1 point
A private school requiring testing and character references for kindergartners	2 points
A private school requiring testing, character references and the mortgage on your house	3 points

By the time my child was one, he or she could:

Say "Ma-ma" or "Da-da"	1 point
Recognize pictures of family members in a photo album	1 point
Read the collected works of James Joyce	2 points

Is your child a superchild? You could take the time to add up the points, but don't bother. Take this one final test and you'll know for sure just how far gone your child really is.

Ask him or her one simple question.

"How are you?"

If your child needs to boot up the computer to come up with an answer, you're in trouble.

Superchildren. Not so long ago, I stumbled across what now looks like a curse to me, in Grant's baby book.

"Mother's greatest aspiration for baby . . . to be everything he can be." Then, as an afterthought, "And to be happy."

When I wrote that, I didn't realize that I had given him a legacy as inevitable as the color of our eyes (tiger green) and the shape of our faces (round): *stress*. A legacy of stress.

During Grant's first three or four years, if you had told me that, I would have laughed you out of the doctor's waiting room. With Grant, I marched into motherhood, certain that I could run my life business as usual, and still have plenty left over. Nothing before had ever stopped me, why should this? A daytime nanny who accompanied me to the office, where I cleverly built an on-site nursery. Throw me any challenge! Run a national contest for a client that required trips across country? I'd pack Grant into my briefcase.

Never mind that I was running on five hours of sleep. My son was growing up with as much love as possible on this planet—and all the advantages.

Then someone told me about babygym. Babygym was offered only during the day. During working hours. And, someone told me, babygym was the only way you could make sure your child could walk the balance beam backward by the age of three—a requirement of entry into the nursery school of choice.

In begged for, borrowed and stolen hours, I began collecting an alphabet soup of advantages. We spent so much time in the car—between classes—that baby Grant learned to recognize the back of my head, as viewed from his baby seat in the rear, more readily than my face.

When I was with Grant, I felt I should be working; when I was working, I felt I should be with Grant. When I tried to do both at the same time, I burped the clients and took Grant to lunch.

Over the years, I inched my way back to a truce with guilt. Just enough time at work, just enough with Grant, all painstakingly calculated to the millisecond. One unaccounted for trip to the pediatrician could throw the whole thing into a frenzy.

So, of course, Grant developed allergies. The kind of indefinable allergies that make a career out of patch tests and shots.

There was no time for allergies in our busy schedule. But there they were.

The pediatrician, an old-fashioned black-bag type, sat me down. Moment of Truth.

"How are you?"

I'm sure the patients in the other rooms thought the worst when I burst out into tears right then and there, crying all over his white coat. To alleviate Grant's symptoms, he prescribed a strong decongestant. For mine, he gave me a book called *How to Talk So Kids Will Listen and Listen So Kids Will Talk*.

As I waited for the water to boil, at stoplights, as the curling iron heated up, I gobbled the wisdom of authors Adele Faber and Elaine Mazlish. Inspired, I came to realize that a loving relationship with your child takes more than love. It takes respect, and appreciation of the fact that the smaller person is capable of having a set of feelings different from yours. That neither you nor your child have right or wrong feelings. You each feel what you feel.

I thought I understood. By cutting back from work and enrolling Grant in everything that moved, I had demonstrated with devotion worthy of a superwoman that I could not do enough for Grant. All I asked in return was that he do everything I told him to do without question. Not that I didn't care about his feelings—there just wasn't enough time. Not if we were going to get to gymnastics on time.

The night I finished reading the book, however, Grant came to my bed with a stomachache. As always, I hugged him and offered to run a warm bath. He didn't want a bath. I suggested a glass of warm milk. He didn't want that, either. I thought of various medicines . . . but then something occurred to me. I asked him if he wanted to talk. We went back to his bed and talked most of the night.

Without even realizing it, I had felt shut out of Grant's life for as long as I could remember. We spent a lot of time together, but I understood that I didn't really know how he felt about things. I knew when he was angry—throwing a tantrum and all. But feelings?

Every day I asked him what he did at school, and he

would say he couldn't remember. It never even occurred to me to ask, "How are you? How's the person Grant, right now? What are you experiencing today?" Not a report card of accomplishments. The sharing of feelings.

Grant told me he was upset that he had to take medicine for his allergies; it made him feel sleepy. Then it hit me like a gong. I was afraid all the time the allergies were emotional—that they were proof that I wasn't a good enough mother. I felt incapable of getting through to Grant, but I hadn't even tried the one thing I knew would work. Sharing myself with him first. My sadness about what he was going through—my fear.

"When you don't share yourself with me, I feel left out. Sad," I said.

Grant asked if he could stop taking the medicine. I felt fear—fear of what the doctor would say. Instead of shutting down, I admitted this to Grant and he opened his heart to me.

"We could ask the doctor if I could just try it, Mom, and see if I do all right. You don't have to be afraid. You'll see."

I felt heard. Connected. He was there for me, and I for him. I finally realized my greatest wish for him. Not to be everything he could be. Something far more important than that . . . to love himself.

Experiment Number Ten

Setup

The allergies cleared up, and with them, many of the misconceptions I held about quality time. Quality time is one of those myths handed to us by women's magazines, eager to help us cope, manage and juggle. What we really long for is not quality time, but quality relationships.

One of the elements of a quality relationship is the ability to surrender part of yourself to the other person. Most superwomen think of quality time as finding something fun or interesting for you and your child to do together. Here is an alternative: a simple experiment that may ask far more of you than you have ever given, yet be infinitely more satisfying to your child in just fifteen minutes.

The Experiment

Find a timer. Set it for fifteen minutes. Now, tell your child that, for these fifteen minutes, you will do anything and everything he or she asks you to do (as long as it is legal and safe).

Analysis

The friend who told me about this said that for the first few months of this game, her daughter Hilary asked her to jump off the fireplace onto the rug and pretend to swim for fifteen minutes. Jump and swim, jump and swim. Grant likes to play hotel. We take turns ordering a pretend room service, with imaginary concoctions brought in by an assortment of snobby bellboys.

As a result of this game, I have come to think of my relationship with my children in terms of "empty" or "full" rather than of "quality time." Fifteen minutes of this kind of surrender is completely satisfying to both of us because I have given myself to be present in my child's world.

Rather than rush our children to "all the advantages," I try to share myself with them whenever we are together. Making a salad for dinner can be a social, aesthetic and sometimes even culinary experience. Rather than shuttle our children to professionals for lessons on every subject in the encyclopedia, we share what we can from our own talent bank of accomplishments. Teaching Grant to blow a clarinet, capture the sounds of his moods on the piano. . . .

When I am exhausted, at the end of the day, I don't worry that he and Jody may be missing out on some enhanced cultural learning experience . . . a concert, or storytime at the library. We flop on some huge pillows and mess around.

As you might expect, you can't always tell the difference between a superchild and a great child from the outside. What is the deciding factor in children—as in their mothers—is strictly internal. Where is the motivation for activity coming from? From mom's idea of what success should look like for the child? From the school's? Or how about from George Lucas? Or is the source the child's own innate desire to grow and achieve? Does the child even remember his or her own natural desires? A baby doesn't think about how badly he or she needs to learn to walk. Doesn't worry about whether she can do it, or when she will. She wants to walk— and eventually, despite our hysteria on the subject—she does.

Or by the time they are two or three years old, have they been programmed, directed and rushed with such velocity to gymnastics and ballet that they come to believe that they were born with toe shoes glued to their feet?

Giving a child the space to explore his or her own ambitions takes courage on the parent's part. What if you give your child more freedom, and he chooses to grow up to be a boob tube addict? We're talking subtleties here. Let me assure you, I would eat my typewriter before I would allow either of my children to grow up couch potatoes. There are lines to be drawn—but where do the parent's values and desires interact and ultimately, simultaneously, respect yet limit the child's own tendencies?

My greatest fear is that, if left to his own, Grant will turn the television on for Saturday morning cartoons sometime in 1986 to finally turn the set off in time for the turn of the century. In truth, on the one occasion that an indulgent baby-sitter let Saturday morning television go unchecked, Grant admitted that he watched seven shows before succumbing to mind-o-mortis. When I arrived home, he was busy building a carnival out of cardboard boxes.

Five shows a week is one of the limits we set. (The useful thing about this setup is that it creates artificial value for purposes of negotiation and bribery, similar to cigarettes in the penitentiary. By adding or taking away a show, we gain leverage throughout the week when we need it.)

Grant is also required to do his homework, brush his teeth and refrain from eating cookies until after dinner. But even superwomen have this stuff down pat. Where we separate the hard-core superwomen from recovering superwomen is in the area of extracurricular activities. Grant can pick one or two at a time. Once he chooses his activity, he must stay with it the entire cycle (semester, season, etc.). Through this, we have created a vehicle for both dialog and commitment. Grant has learned that he can't have it all. Instead, he can have what he wants most (usually). Together, we explore the options—list the pros and cons. Observe classes and discuss the benefits and consequences of involvement. When he finally chooses, he gives his all. His choice is not just another activity in a meaningless list of obligations. It is his choice. When he makes a mistake—chooses something that turns out to be boring or difficult—he sticks it out to the end. He learns discipline and responsibility.

When you think about it, which is the greater gift you can give your child . . . to give her or him all the advantages? Or to help them develop the ability to make wise choices?

All this is well and fine, until Grant has made his commitment to acting class, and all the boys in his schoolroom choose to play soccer.

And here's my definition of a great child.

"Grant, how do you feel with all the boys in your class on teams and you're not?"

"They're not all playing soccer. Mat's not."

"Don't you feel left out? Do they say mean things?"

"Why? Last year, my team won second place. I know I can play soccer if I want. But to me, it just feels like running back and forth and back and forth. I like acting."

Grant's soccer season was instructive to me. I did not like how mad I got when they disqualified the goal Grant made. In fact, I wanted to kill. In fact, just about every adult there wanted to kill. On the other hand, every child—with the exception of the coach's son—appeared to prefer to pick and blow the dandelions. Basically, the game consisted of son of coach kicking goals while the parents hurled fearsome threats and passionate entreaties to their little ones—desperate attempts from the sidelines to get their sons' eyes off the clouds, the grass, the cartons of lemonade and onto the ball. In fact, it was they—the children—who should have been entreating us to take time to smell the roses. Children understand the value of daydreaming. They understand the time and place for silliness and for play without purpose. They can be excellent teachers. In fact, they are so good at it, that if you do not have a child of your own, you should borrow one and begin to learn.

Chapter Fourteen

WHOSE LIFE IS IT, ANYWAY?

Fantasy day. I awake to dancercize around the living room to my favorite record. When I finish, my husband has breakfast cooking. My children give me big hugs, showing me how nicely they've dressed. Off to school and daycare you go, little ones! Mommy is going downstairs to write the new Great American Novel!

Real day. My boy is looking for his lost shoe, complaining that I make him dress before breakfast. If I don't, however, he will eat a leisurely four courses rather than gulping his muffins like the rest of us, and he'll be a half hour late for school. My girl isn't dressed, either. But since she's only one year old, it's forgivable. Husband is already off at work and I should be. Except that today is the day I take the Big One. The Day Just for Me.

The pressure is on. 9:30, kids delivered, and I haven't

decided yet whether the Day Just for Me leans more toward completing chapter one of my opus or getting the right flicker of my car fixed. What good will chapter one of my Great American Novel be, if the next time I leave the house to buy groceries a huge truck doesn't see my signal because the flicker is broken and I end up in the hospital? On the other hand, perhaps I am just procrastinating.

Okay—the clock is ticking away *my* fantasy day. Start anywhere! Start dancing! Okay. Here I am doing something terrific for myself. Huffing and puffing now to my favorite record. Thinking about how sooner or later the effort is bound to reach the subterranean reaches where cellulite is formed. How proud my husband would be of me. What a good role model I am for my children. And I am hating every minute of it.

All of a sudden, for no particular reason, I hear the music, remember that my body is moving. I feel my legs stretching, my arms reaching—and I realize that the physical sensations I am experiencing, the intermingling of pain and pleasure, feel good. For five minutes—maybe ten—I forget to watch the hands of the clock. I even forget to think about the fact that what I am doing is good for me. I am just doing it and having the time of my life at it. Then the song ends. Like one of Pavlov's hounds, I go back to huffing and puffing, muttering about the sweat and scratching aerobics off my good-things-to-do-for-myself-today list.

So here's the point. I was already three hours into My Day, and I'd only managed five minutes that contained any of the quality of my fantasy. Whether my children and husband were home—and here's the painful part—or not!

A few minutes later into My Special Day, self-consciously drinking a cup of My Special Coffee, I pondered this. Realizing that perhaps the thing of note is not the lost three hours. But rather, the miracle of the found minutes. I'd had five minutes this day that I'd actually been living my own life. I finished my coffee, discovering that nobody was watching, waiting to congratulate me for remembering to sip slowly. I was now into hour four of My Day Just for Me. As I pondered the enormity of what lay ahead—an expedition to the typewriter, lunch, time to read or take a hot bath—I realized that I would be content with a more modest goal: five more minutes knowing I was living my own life. Whether or not my flicker is broken.

It is no simple task to live your own life. It is far easier to pack your schedule so tight with busy, productive activities that you do not have to confront the feeling of emptiness you hold inside. Emptiness that is inevitable when you neglect to take the time and risks involved with such qualities of life as vulnerability, compassion, intimacy and love. Tender virtues, squashed by the hobnailed boots that rush our children from lesson to lesson—their little legs chugging as fast as they can go to keep up with our frantic pace. Husbands and wives, entertaining, complaining or ignoring each other. Busy, busy, busy we pass the days of our lives—gone all too soon. Gone before we get to our dreams of creative expression, self-fulfillment, nurturing. Remembering that we care about sunrises and sunsets. Scrambling for bigger houses, more digits in our incomes, never stopping to enjoy the riches that came to us—without struggle or effort—with birth. Waves on the ocean, a single daisy, a redwood forest. Not to mention each other. The potential we contain—individually and together—for exploration, for adventure, for joy! For all of us, sooner or later, there are moments—windows—when the busyness cracks and we get a glimpse of what's going on underneath. For many, divorce provides a window. Major illness for some, death for all. There are lesser opportunities, as well. Like when we sold our dream house, and the financing for the cottage had not come through yet. Stripped of the roof, walls and carpeting that usually box our reality into a neat, little package, we felt lost for a while. Between jobs—that's another good one.

We look at these cataclysmic moments as disasters. What

they are is windows. We see who we are, stripped momentarily of the roles, goods and relationships that have determined who we thought we were. The fear, the discomfort we feel at such moments is merely an amplification of what you faced in Experiment Number One: the five-minute experience of doing nothing.

For previous generations, struggling through a depression and a war, there was no alternative to the business of survival. Many of us, however, are at a point in history when it is possible to borrow time from our life-styles of coping, balancing and juggling to lay claim to what I believe to be our next great frontier: what lies beneath the surface of ourselves. The miracle for us is that we can choose to do so without needing to wait for a crisis to make such an exploration mandatory. Embarking on this journey, answering the question, "Whose life is it, anyway?" is, in my opinion, not only our luxury, but our obligation. We are here for a purpose. It is the responsibility of every one of us to discover what our own special song may be—and to sing it. A chorus of voices, each blending together in harmony. That is my vision. That is my song.

Until recently, if you had asked me about the meaning of life, I would have been very clear. It was, simply, this: to lose ten pounds.

I hung out most of my life being obsessed with those same extra ten pounds. I made a career out of them. In retrospect, I realize how grateful I am to them.

In my early years, they shielded me from pain and vulnerability I did not yet know how to handle. Everything that went wrong was the pounds' fault. They never complained about it—they took the blame quietly, going on about their business as I went about mine. Over time I began to realize that I could do something about them. When I was unable yet to bring what I needed to make things happen in the world around me, I could make the pounds go away. In fact, this became such an important lesson for me that I did so—over and over again. Moving the clock ahead once again, I realized that I no longer needed weight loss to prove my effectiveness. I resolved to let them go once and for all. But suddenly, they would not budge.

Diets that had always worked like a charm began to fail. Glassy-eyed, I stripped book and drugstore shelves bare—searching for the solution, and failing time and time again. Finally, I took the step that began the process that resulted, ultimately, in Superwomen's Anonymous: I gave up on external solutions and began to look within.

I looked at issues relating to my own self-esteem. My belief that I did not deserve to have what I wanted. I realized that, for me, having my ideal weight was the prize that I would award myself someday—but only when I had everything else mastered first: my prize for being perfect. When I fell short, I stifled the feelings of inadequacy with food and with busyness.

When I marched my body into karate, I felt old and fat and out of shape. All I had, as a matter of fact, was courage. I determined that I would not let my own disparaging opinions about myself stop me from getting what I truly deserved ever again. One of the things I deserve is a fit body. And so, I dragged myself time after time. I was the worst in the class, mostly because I was so busy looking into the mirror thinking about how terrible I was doing instead of looking at the sensei who patiently, over and over again, corrected my mistakes. Without judgment, with compassion. I, who had never stayed with anything that I couldn't be best at, persisted. I came home more than once in tears, droplets dripping off my nose as I practiced Kata, the movements that form the basis for the system I was studying. The system I was learning. Before long, I realized that my fat, old body was doing all kinds of things I'd never imagined possible. Things like 100 sit-ups, some incredible contortion accurately called tiger bends, and enough kata to get me first a green belt and then a purple. One day I realized that I was watching my sensei demonstrate a new kata—and the critical voice was gone. I was there, present with myself. My body was still not my ideal—but I had a newfound respect for it, and for myself. It was not my dream body, but it was mine. And now, after all these years, I was respecting it and respecting myself because I did deserve, I do deserve and I have always deserved—whether I knew it or not—to have what I want.

I studied karate for several years, through the birth of my daughter, and back again to complete my goal. I wanted a brown belt. To me, that would have meant that I cared enough about myself to be the worst in the class. To have persisted through all the considerations to do something I really wanted for myself. When I finally did get my belt, I realized that I was now ready to apply the same commitment to anything I could ever want to accomplish in my life.

Out of this realization, I began to look at my life the way a kid feels in a candy store . . . with a handful of change. Write a novel? I want that! Okay, make the space for that. Beauty? What will that take? More frequent visits to my hairdresser? Facials? I'm worth it.

Some of the choices came easily. Dan had no problem watching the kids a couple of mornings a week so I could row. I'd just never asked. Others called forth a great deal of pain. Like my realization that I wanted to sell the house to make room financially and emotionally for creativity, adventure and relaxation.

At times, as I moved forward through my life, I felt that I had succeeded only in creating bigger problems for myself. As I let go of the old, and the new had not yet come into focus, I either remembered to climb down—or simply fell—into more than one black void. I have not always handled these moments with as much grace or perspective as one would hope for. I have not, on the other hand, come anywhere close to becoming a bag lady. Often feeling like a five-legged horse, I keep trotting on what Scott Peck calls "the road less traveled." I keep finding new adventures, new surprises and new pains. As my husband—cotraveler and companion—reminds me, I deserve it all.

Regardless of the fact that I am busier than ever at this exact moment in time, I am relatively certain that I am not on the Superwoman's Le Mans anymore. If I'm on open road, I am still too often traveling at breakneck speed. I have, however, surrounded myself with plenty of people who are more than willing to remind me to stop to smell the roses.

There's Christine, my phone buddy. We start every weekday morning with a 6:30 A.M. phone call, sharing our wins and our goals for the day. We have seen each other through more than a year of tumultuous change in our lives. Having declared ourselves, we are each the keeper of the other's vision: providing that much more perspective and memory at the start of each new day. We remind each other that we deserve to have what we want, and we remember to stop and acknowledge ourselves when we do.

There are Cathy and Mary, my adventure pals. We get together for an afternoon every other week just to have fun. Remember playing with your classmates in elementary school? Hanging out with your girlfriends in high school? We three are specifically re-creating the joy and adventure of life, as we take turns leading the others on adventures. We've walked together through huge redwood groves, played with waves at the ocean and tried our hand at making serving trays out of wood.

There are my mom and dad, thoroughly enjoying the simplicity of their retirement—sharing it enthusiastically as a gift to my entire family. Not only the special apples, selected with great care at the farmer's market down the road. But the moments of connection, devoid of any overt purpose. I enjoy seeing Mom and Dad; telling Grant ghost stories by flashlight beneath a jury-rigged tent made of sheets and pillow cases; lifting Jody to bring her closer to the pictures on the walls, sharing the gift of discovery of colors and shapes.

There's Grant, who, like most children, is so willing to teach me the lesson of forgiveness. And Jody, who reminds me of the potential I, too, came here with. The capacity for joy, for vitality, for appreciation and for love. She and I are now both so willing.

And Dan. Who has ridden his relationship with me for seventeen years, more often than not on a slippery horse with no saddle. Having let go at last of the fact that we cannot possibly do or be everything to the other, we have begun a far richer journey—exploring side by side the meaning of love, of vulnerability and of intimacy.

Now, in addition to my garden of friends and family, I have 2000 members of Superwomen's Anonymous: women and the men who care about them, who have been willing to share their journey with me. I have their letters, scrawled in bold print, typed by a secretary, neatly printed with perfumed ink to remind me that I—that *we*—are exploring the next frontier. For all of us, I have another experiment.

_____*Experiment Number Twelve*_____

Setup:

Before I end this handbook, I want to open the space for you to give yourself the greatest gift of all.

The Experiment:

Stand in front of a mirror. Take in what you see. Do you have judgments about her? Are there things you feel she doesn't deserve? Let your mind run through its thoughts for a while, knowing that you will soon short-circuit the wiring. For now, as you look at this reflection, imagine that your image is being reflected on the surface of a crystal-clear pond of water. Liquid, fluid. Now, imagine yourself falling in. Surrender to the sensation, embrace the feeling. When you are satiated, step away from the mirror—but take the feeling with you.

Analysis

This is your life, now live it!

Chapter Fifteen.

THE THEORY OF OPTIMISTIC EVOLUTION

When I began my own journey some time ago, I had no idea where I was going. I did not know if anybody would come with me, or who, if anybody, I was liable to encounter along the way. All I knew was that, if I did not explore unknown terrain, I was clearly in danger that my life would forever remain frozen in ice: a never-ending gray sameness that accompanied my fifty-hour work weeks, exhausted routines and relationships. My grace is that hopelessness bore for me a kind of reckless courage. I did not know what lay ahead, but I was certain of what lay behind. It had been a long time since I had felt inspired, centered, serene or happy. It had been so long, as a matter of fact, that while I thought I knew what these experiences would feel like, I had—in actuality—forgotten. That happiness was like a long-gone French pastry. I could picture the fine layers, remember the delicate texture, but could not re-create the taste. I had let both the French pastry and my happiness out of my life so long ago, I couldn't remember either enough to be enticed by them.

As I continued on my journey, I caught an occasional whiff of something wonderful baking in long-forgotten ovens. Whenever I did, my pace quickened. At the door to the kitchen, I eagerly dipped my finger in the frosting bowl: ecstatic at the first taste, eager for it to finish baking. And then, at last, I had it. Intoxicated with the experience, my motivation subtly shifted. At this point, I stopped saying enough is enough to the things I didn't want to run my life anymore. I started to say yes to the things I did want.

On the other side of the void, there are incredible joys— moments of ecstasy so wondrous that you will know that every truth you face up to, every bit of programming you painfully shed, every courageous step you take is worth it. Even in the midst of battling with old decisions, old patterns, you know you are equipped with the tools and the motivation to live your life the best way you know how—not perfectly, maybe, but in an even better way: to the fullest.

Finally, in order to live as I had been, I had no choice but to unwillingly trust that, if I kept checking into myself for guidance, I would stay on the path. I kept waiting for an ax to fall—but it never did. There were some touch-and-go moments, but I got to know my own strength and courage well.

Along the way, I shined my lantern into the night, to see if there might be any more like myself. I plunged forward, trusting only that my feeling of inadequacy was not personal, but rather something shared by women throughout my friendship and business circles, throughout the city, the state . . . maybe even the world. I took a deep breath and stated publicly what had been brewing over coffee with my husband and a few dear friends. It's a message that is now being passed from person to person around the world. Now, not only are there lots of lanterns shining in the night, there are klieg lights—all the excitement of opening night. Opening night of a new decade that is simply starting a little late. I am optimistic about superwomen, about our generation, and about our world. Every day now, I have the privilege of meeting people who are inspirational to me. People like a well-known deejay with one of our local radio stations. When he called me to be on his show, I realized that I hadn't heard his name for a while. When I saw him, I thought from his looks—the clear, calm eyes, the easy smile—that he'd gone on a round-the-world cruise. What he had done, at age thirty-eight, was suffer a massive heart attack. Being a deejay is one of the more stressful jobs. Yet there he was, getting the next record on the turntable with one hand, cueing up the next commercial with another, signaling to the engineer at the controls with his head, and carrying on a wonderful conversation with me.

I asked if he had always been like this, and he laughed so loud the engineer had to adjust the levels.

"Are you kidding, I was one of the most uptight jockeys in town," he explained. "I was always running to catch up, spilling coffee on my notes, so busy wiping up I'd miss my on-air cue. Then I'd beat myself up for an hour or two for having made a mistake."

"What happened?"

"When I first felt the grips of pain in my chest, I felt relieved in a funny kind of way. Maybe I'd found a way out of the stress of my life. When I came out of it, lying there in the hospital, hooked up to a bunch of machines that were working overtime to keep me alive, I realized how desperate I had been. That even death would have been an acceptable solution to the emptiness I'd been feeling. But everyday, my wife and kids came. I had time to think, to talk to them, to see how much they wanted me to live. I'd almost bit the big one—left them behind, without ever really getting to know them. When I finally turned the corner, I realized what a gift life is. I thought long and hard about getting back into radio. There's plenty of us with health, drug and alcohol problems in this field. Could I handle the pressure? Then I remembered why I'd gotten into radio in the first place. It's fun! Punching up the music, having thousands of invisible people laugh at your jokes, meeting people like you. I decided to come back, but vowed to leave the day I started to take this too seriously. I see we're on standby now. Ready for the first question?"

I would have been speechless with awe, had he not crafted his interview so beautifully. With his heartfelt understanding of the kinds of things I had discovered, we discussed the miracle of our generation. That we have the incredible luxury—unlike generations of the past and many people that even today are still struggling with issues of survival—to explore the frontiers of what lies beneath the surface of our life-styles of coping, balancing and juggling. More and more of us are doing so, even at times when there is no particular crisis at hand. We have somehow mustered the courage to look inward, even knowing that we are liable to encounter all kinds of surprises—some not so pleasant.

In the sixties, we created love-ins and women's liberation. In the eighties, we can once again flex our muscles to wake up our generation first, and then the world, to an expanded universe of possibilities. I believe that the enormous response to my message is the beginning of a new era of creativity, excitement and optimism for us all: the rebirth of choice and freedom. The evolution of our society into a greenhouse for creativity, compassion and the kind of vulnerability that reflects an understanding of what it means to be truly powerful. I believe that the reception to my ideas indicates that society is ready to take the next step in its evolution: one that will benefit every person, every country, every continent in the world.

PART IV

Declarations

FROM SUPERWOMEN TO GREAT WOMEN

_____ *The Journey Has Begun* _____

Presented here is a sampling of the more than 2000 letters that have been sent to Superwomen's Anonymous from around the world. In many cases, these correspondents had to go to great lengths to find our address. Not a penny of paid advertising supported our communication. The message has been passed by word of mouth and through individuals in the media who felt moved to share it. Together these letters create a composite of what it is like to be a "role model" in our society today.

I have not created the insight, the dedication and the inspiration evidenced in these letters—I have merely tapped into it. If some spirit has now been given permission to surface, I salute all of us who are willing for this moment to at long last arrive. As one of my members wrote, "Read and weep . . . or smile. It's up to all of us."

Hello Carol,

A friend from Indianapolis recently sent me information about Superwomen's Anonymous. I got the article just in time.

I picked up my mail on the way to an evening TV interview. After the interview, I had to catch a late flight out to Philadelphia so I would arrive in time for a morning meeting. At the airport, I was reading my mail as I walked down the stairs. After all, why should a superwoman take the escalator when she can tone up her thighs by taking the stairs? Why should she waste time just walking down stairs when she can read her mail and touch up her lipstick at the same time? Anyhow, as I was reading your article, walking down the stairs and touching up my lipstick, I made one graceless trip to the bottom of the stairs. I took a brief moment to reflect upon what I was reading, laugh to myself, regain my composure and then dash for the ticket counter.

I did make my plane to Philadelphia for the morning meeting. I made my afternoon meeting in Boston. I was right on time for my evening dinner with a friend in New York. Thanks to you, I didn't clean my house when I arrived home at 3:00 A.M.

I admit I may not be able to totally surrender my superwoman attitude. But at least I've got a start.

Enjoy Today!
J. Fox
Clearwater, Florida

Dear Anon,

One morning last week I set the alarm for 5:15 A.M., so that I could iron my nylons and fix a nourishing breakfast for the cats before arriving fifteen minutes early for the Mayor's State of the City Breakfast at 7:15 A.M. I grabbed a newspaper on the way to my table to read it surreptitiously between bites. Sometime during the report on city cesspools, I discovered the article about Superwomen's Anonymous. I must tell you that it made my day.

I finished reading the article at red lights on my way to the office. By the time I had picked up the dry cleaning and polished my shoes while dictating morning correspondence into a portable tape recorder, I knew that I had to apply for membership, even if to be rejected.

As desperate as I am to become a member of SWA, I think it only fair to tell you that you may not find me acceptable because of my inability to make a full commitment at one fell swoop. Although I have no trouble at all giving up the briefcase, closed-toe pumps and my "aggression" home study tapes, I find that I am still hopelessly addicted to dangerously excessive aerobicization and to outrageously usurious house payments. However, on my behalf, I have noticed that my earrings now dangle, my broken hair dryer has not been replaced, and I haven't had the urge to take a man to dinner on my American Express Card for several weeks.

Betty A. Kennedy
Assistant District Attorney
San Bernardino County, California

Dear Carol,

A very timely article on you woke me up to the fact that women have been separately trying to discover what has gone wrong with their superwoman image. (If they can get off the treadmill long enough to contemplate it.) It seems that what women are allowed to do (i.e., new careers) has changed in the last few years, but the basic structure (i.e., what has been expected in the past) has not.

So all we have done is take on more work with no extra pay or emotional support. It sure is time to re-evaluate.

I applaud you for trying to make women aware that other women are having the same problems coping with being a superwoman. Once we start discussing it among ourselves and realize it is not a solitary problem, I am sure we will come up with new and exciting solutions, as you did in your life.

I am going down to South Carolina to do free-lance work as a mill person and get off the eight-to-five grind I've been on since 1977. I am pooped. But my solution is exciting! So there you have it.

Jane Triplett
Columbia, South Carolina

Dear Ms. Orsborn:

We live in a time when we are inundated by ads proclaiming the wonders of women who enter marathons, open shows at the local gallery, raise 2.5 children (who, in turn, write letters to world leaders and enter Purdue at sixteen), keep up with the latest novels, volunteer for several organizations, model in their off hours and prepare gourmet fetes.

I am but twenty-three, working in an advertising agency,

paying back student loans and volunteering for literacy—
yet, already I am experiencing the frustration of the superwoman media hype. Nothing seems to be enough and I
often feel as though my time is never mine. There's a cloud
of guilt that hangs off center over my shoulder: I should be
doing more. I should accomplish more. I should be more. I
should . . . the list is endless.

I resent the whole superwoman profile that a number of
media sources have imposed upon me and the women
around me.

Enough *is* enough.

Most Sincerely,
LeAnne M. Wawrzaszek
Winter Springs, Florida

Dear Carol Orsborn:

I am writing this letter for my sister, age seventy-two
young. Her first thought was the same as mine. We are
concerned about our daughters. My sister and I agree that
our children's generation will never reach the age we have.
They are likely to not even make fifty at the pace they are
going. Life is beautiful. There is so much to see and do—but
at a slower pace.

Thank You,
Stella Walsh

Superwomen's Anonymous:

I am the mother of a two-year-old boy whom I love dearly (most of the time). I am also a full-time employee at NYC Presbyterian Hospital. My job is a rewarding one because I have to use my brain. However, it is very demanding, as I don't stop from the minute I get there until I go home. Into the picture comes my son, when I get home. I am sometimes tired and want to unwind, but "Danny" wants Mommy to do this and that, and it's very trying when I'm tired. My husband goes to school three nights a week and works six days a week, and is totally "out of it."

I feel so burned out in every aspect of my existence and I don't know what to do. I feel like *enough is enough*. I want to enjoy my life with my son and husband, and feel if I had a part-time job, it would make a world of difference for me. I want to be proud of what I do both at work and at home.

Sincerely,
Kathy Jordan
New York, New York

Love your philosophy!

After working part-time for seven years, I decided to "live up to my potential" and took a full-time job with a software company. We had just moved our family to North Carolina. We built a new home and helped our three teenage sons adjust. Within seven months, I had mono—at 43!

I am firmly commited to gearing down. Enough is enough.

Marsha Ambrose
Cary, North Carolina

Dear Carol:

I came very close to where you were when I realized I was literally killing myself. I'm thirty-eight years old and own a training and consulting firm with eighteen associates in two states. We grossed over a half million last year, with expectations of nearly doubling that this year. I'm happily married and we're raising a three-year-old, a one-year-old and one is on the way. I'm very tied to family commitments, as we have three senior persons over ninety years old in our family. I worked fifty–sixty hours a week until Christmas, when I said, "Enough is enough."

Now I read one hour for *me* every night after the children are in bed, and I'm beginning to explore other ways to rediscover myself and my relationship with my husband.

Congratulations to you for discovering that business is to support family, not the reverse.

Best,
Marcey Ellen Uday

Dear Ex-Superwomen—

Thanks for making today special. Now I can comfortably make out tomorrow's list of Things to Do and will *not* add things I've already done just so I can check 'em off and look more efficient.

Involvement is educational . . . it's fun . . . it's challenging . . . and it's exhausting. I enjoy everything I do, but there must be a time a bell rings and I say, "Enough is enough."

Sincerely,
Shirley Brickman
Atlanta, Georgia

Carol—

Thank you! Being a bright, creative, rather active and somewhat educated woman, I'm tired of being told that if I ever get my act together or focus on one thing, I'll really get somewhere. Thanks, but I'm already where I am, and that's where I'm going, and that's enough.

My biggest challenge is learning to simplify while maintaining the diversity of my interests to the depth that brings me such satisfaction. My resolution is not a mandate for change, but a statement affirming me as already, what— "sufficient?" That is, "I don't have to explain myself to anybody."

Enough.

Love,
Mary Marks
Pasadena, California

Dear Mrs. Orsborn:

The older I get, the more I realize that what matters most in life are the so-called "spiritual values" and human relationships. Now that my children are all grown up, I am taking it easy and enjoying life. No more working two jobs and all the overtime I can get. I paint and visit friends and try to do a little extra for other people. But I see people I know and love who are working harder than ever, ruining their dispositions and probably their health in the process, for the gain of material things and so-called "security."

The other nurses I work with (I'm an RN) are all in school, going for their BSs or masters', for more prestige and more money, but will it make them better at the patients' bedsides? I think not. Many times they are so tired because of their own schedules, that they don't have anything left over to give to their patients. I don't want to be that way. If you are racing around trying to be a super nurse, you don't have time to cheer up the patients.

Thank you!
Dian Allison
Montrose California

Dear "Supe,"

I am fifty (just), and have spent the last thirty years being an SW:

Stats: mother of four boys, a creative director at American Greetings, President of a local theater group, wife of a truly nice man, etc., etc., ad forever. . . .

Real me: painter, writer, actress, dreamer.

This year, I decided to resolve this dichotomy:

1. To approach my boss with a job concept: to abandon my managerial duties and develop a concept group. (Surprisingly: accepted.)
2. To not renew my presidency of the theater group, and devote my time to building a season of original scripts. (Cheers all around.)
3. To set up a working studio in one of the emptied nests upstairs and start "waking up" the creative synapses. (I.e., art directing *myself* for a change!)
4. To stop volunteering for everything that presented itself and (this is no small thing):
5. To assign all the Thanksgiving diners a responsibility for a portion of the meal . . . including dishes.

I considered rowing a boat out into Lake Erie for inspiration, but somehow it's not the same. . . .

Onward. . . .

I'm sure that some of my new endeavors will be just as strenuous and foolhardy as the ones I traded in, but they are *mine*!

Thanks,
Barbara Brown
North Olmsted, Ohio

To Carol Orsborn:

Up until a year ago, I worked an eighty-hour week year-round as a teacher/writer/lecturer/mother/wife. My specialties as a professor and critic at Penn State Behrend College were, and sometimes still are, poetry, women's studies and feminist criticism, psychoanalytic theory, and American attitudes toward death. About four years ago, I looked in the mirror (seriously now, I really did) and asked myself what a fundamentally sane woman like me was doing in the academic fast lane, making myself old and half crazy before it was absolutely necessary. I set out to change it all, and I made it (I think), but it took three years.

Now I live more or less like a human being most of the time. Sometimes I do fall off the wagon and go on a work binge for a few weeks. Sooner or later I'll have to accept the fact that I'm one of those people who should never do even one sixteen-hour workday. It only leads to another and another and another, and before I know it, I'm juggling three schedule books at once, and passing members of my family on my way to an appointment, with a kiss-kiss-luvya-you're-marvelous-stay-that-way-ciao look on my face as I walk out the door. And when that mentality takes over, it sometimes takes weeks for someone who loves me to penetrate the urethane coating so as to point out to me that, while I've been beyond human reach on a toot, the seasons have changed, the dog has died, and he himself has aged considerably while waiting for me to get home for dinner. Because, contrary to the notion superwomen have that we are all things to all people, we often fail everybody, especially our own best selves, in the effort.

So, at last, Superwomen's Anonymous to my rescue, to lend support and give me courage when I'm in danger of saying yes to that latest invitation to present a professional paper in Paris or Steubenville, which sounds like a good idea at the time but will really turn into just one more obligation that keeps me from living my life. (Sorry, life's over. Time's up. Aw. That was too quick, no fair. Don't I get another one? Nope.)

Sincerely,
Dr. Diana Hume George
Erie, Pennsylvania

Dear SWA:

You mean I'm not guilty for taking a five-minute breather?

Roberta Sterling
New York, New York

PART V

Epilogue

_____*Epilogue*_____

FOUR WEEKS A.D.*

One irony of this book's existence has most probably not passed you by. That is, that I have spent the last four months writing about the joys of doing things like floating serenely on the Bay—while crashing against the most demanding deadlines of my life. I have done so while continuing to run my business (admittedly reduced in size), meet my family's demands (not reduced in size), and turn out an issue of the Superwomen's Anonymous newsletter—that seemingly "fun thing to do" that inadvertently spawned my return engagement to superwomandom.

* After Delivery (of Body of Book to Publisher)

But there has been a difference for me this time. I did not even begin to try to cope, manage or juggle. I understood the meaning of making choices and I made them.

There has been an elegant simplicity to single-mindedly investing so much of my energy, thought and attention into this manuscript: relaxed time with family and friends going on temporary hold. Knowing that the choice was mine—blessedly devoid of guilt—I have been free to tap new reservoirs of energy and inspiration.

In the four weeks after finishing *Enough Is Enough*, I have returned to my preferred life-style, which includes time once again for long walks to nowhere and back. Of course, it is Spring. With renewed commitment—and gratitude—I have already beaten my personal best of five minutes of happiness. I have had time to catch up with friends and family, and with the many books and magazines increasingly addressing the superwoman issue that had been stacking up on my bedstand.

I am reminded that there is no single answer for myself—work versus children, for instance—let alone one answer that will work for all of us. Rather, there is the far greater challenge of responding to our individual needs and desires, month by month, moment by moment.

As my editor, Stacy Creamer (who aspires to recovering from superwomanism herself "someday") says, "While it would be nice to stop and smell the roses, that's not all that *Enough Is Enough* is about. Properly understood, what it boils down to is to choose your own occasions to rise to."

In emerging, I am newly struck with the courage we must call upon ourselves to engage in the vulnerability and volatility of transitions. It is painful to run counter to our culture's mass-marketed philosophy that "we should have, do and be it all—even if coping is the best one can achieve as a result." There will always be plenty of people eager to tell us what to believe and do. The same voices that once convinced us to wear saddle shoes in the fifties and love beads in the sixties are happy to oblige us with such specific directions for the eighties as how many children to have, how much to work or not to work, how many miles to jog—and how to feel about yourself if you don't.

I say it's time to get on with it. We are adults now, capable of making our own decisions—for better or for worse. We have to take the time and courage to get to know ourselves better so we can decide these issues for ourselves, on our own. For those of us going for more than coping, this is new terrain yet to be explored. I cast my vote for the end of togetherness for today's women. No more saddle shoes. No more love beads. No more superwomen—and no more whatever's next. Let's explore the boundaries of freedom. Let's blossom into a field of wildflowers—each bud a different option or choice. Let's make vitality, creativity and originality qualities that are valued by society. Let's be wild and wonderful and free!

Let's cry over the tough decisions we've had to make, the roads not taken—but this time, not with bitterness, but with the kind of sweet melancholy that reminds us that greatness is a path for the courageous. It is time to honor ourselves, to recognize our vulnerability and our limitations, to celebrate the nobility of our own choices—each one of us a special voice in the chorale of humanity. Time to try very hard not to impose our preferences on those around us. Time to appreciate the results when decisions work out—and to offer compassion when they do not.

Most of all, it is time to live your own life.

This is not the end, this is enough.

COMMENTARY, RESOURCES AND COMPANIONS

This handbook is written for all of us who are eager to explore an expanded world of opportunities. This handbook is meant to inspire you on your journey, as I have been inspired on mine.

(Alphabetical Listings by Author/Artist)

BRANDEN, NATHANIEL, DR. *The Psychology of Romantic Love* (St. Martin's Press, 1980). Many of us say that a loving relationship is the most important thing to us, yet we spend less time learning what that will take than we do reading the operating manual on our toaster oven. Branden presents a realistic and inspiring vision of what is possible for relationships: one that can function in our lives as one path to self-discovery.

BUZAN, TONY. *Use Both Sides of Your Brain* (E. P. Dutton, 1976). Creative thinking can be expanded through step-by-step exercises. While I absorbed many of the concepts in this book through

my Living Journal coursework with psychologist/creativity consultant Sara Deutsch at the College of Marin, Kentfield, California, this book serves as an excellent overview of the subject.

EDELSTEIN, SALLY. *This Year's Girl* (Dolphin Books, 1985). The
impact of advertising and the media on our culture is enormous.
Through high humor, this book of cutout dolls—accompanied by
several decades of fashion, paraphernalia and kitsch—illustrates
the common experiences women of my generation have shared
from the mid-fifties on. I find it frightening, how many private
memories I thought were my very own have ended up in a book by
a woman I've never met who lives on the other side of the country.

EMERY, STEWART. *The Owner's Manual for Your Life* (Doubleday,
1982). Also, *Actualizations* (Irvington, 1978). The work of Stewart
Emery and partner Carol Augustus, cofounders of Actualizations,
has opened the door for many westerners to the fresh perspective
of other cultures, other philosophies and other psychologies.
Through my studies with them, I was introduced to the thinking of
Maslow and Jung, and given the opportunity to put my awareness
into practice. This particular book leads the reader through our
lives from the womb onward, pointing out how and why we develop self-defeating strategies . . . and shows us how we can cause
joy to blossom again. Either of these books, or Actualizations itself,
are excellent places to start with Emery and Augustus . . . an on-
ramp to the freeway of awareness of the human spirit.

FABER, ADELE, and ELAINE MAZLISH. *How to Talk So Kids Will
Listen and Listen So Kids Will Talk* (Rawson Associates, 1980).
This is a practical book about one of the most important relationships in a parent's life: her children. It addresses itself to everyday problems that parents have to deal with—anger (their own
as well as their children's), neglected household chores, fighting
between the kids, defiance, etc.—and suggests ways of commu-
nicating that help all family members feel good about themselves.

HESSE, HERMAN, *Siddhartha* (New Directions, 1951). This classic
that I first read in high school introduced me to the concept of life
as a spiritual journey. It is the story of a soul's long quest for the

ultimate answer to the enigma of man's role on this earth. Dust off your old copy and read it again. The struggles, the temptations, the heartache that accompanied Siddhartha's journey to self-knowledge may now take on added perspective for you as well.

JAMPOLSKY, GERALD G., M.D. *Love Is Letting Go of Fear* (Celestial Arts, 1979). Lessons to help you let go of fear, replacing it with love. The book points out that, to experience this new reality, we must be willing to let go of our obsession with the past and the future. If we can do this, we are ready to learn how to transform ourselves.

JOEL, BILLY. "Just the Way You Are" (Columbia Records, 1977). This song is the perfect creative expression of acceptance—a prerequisite for love. Next time you hear this song, imagine that you are singing the words to yourself. This will give you a vision of how far you have to go—or have already come.

JUNG, CARL. *Man and His Symbols* (Doubleday, 1969). Written by Jung at the age of eighty-three, this book emphasizes that man can achieve wholeness only through a knowledge and acceptance of the unconscious—a knowledge acquired through dreams and their symbols. Jung says that contemporary man "is blind to the fact that, with all his rationality and efficiency . . . his gods and demons have not disappeared at all; they have merely got new names. They keep him on the run with restlessness, vague apprehensions . . . and, above all, an impressive array of neuroses."

KERR, CHRISTINE. Christine is my phone buddy. I have had an advance peek at her humorous writing. For over a year, I have been privy to her insight and wisdom. Watch for anything by her to be published any time in the future.

KIM, RICHARD. *The Classical Man* (Masters Publication, 1982). Also, *The Weaponless Warriors* (Ohara Publications, 1974). Through my studies with my sensei, Sam Samarrai, I heard many wonderful and inspiring stories about the head of the Zen Bei Butoku-Kai, Richard Kim. Kim studied under some of the great karate masters of the time, sharing much of the history and philosophy of martial arts in his books and his teachings. For those of us brought up in a culture that has emphasized team sports as a model for business relationships, the Eastern philosophies, as represented by the lives of such famous samurai as Miyamoto Musashi, Gichin Funakoshi, Chogun Miyagi and many more, are illuminating.

KRICH, JOHN. *Music in Every Room: Around the World in a Bad Mood* (McGraw-Hill, 1984). A hysterical account of an aging sixties radical-turned-journalist who, with his girlfriend, has come to the Far East in search of Nirvana. This book is on my list for reminding me in black and white that, wherever my dreams may take me—my self, for better or for worse, comes along. If I can't indulge my fantasies for world travel at the moment, it's just as well. I can get myself in shape so that whether or not I am living my vision—with others or alone—I will at least be in good company.

MEIR, GOLDA. *My Life* (G. P. Putnam's Sons, 1975). This inspiring book reveals the greatness that led an individual woman, born in Russia and brought up in Milwaukee, to become the prime minister of Israel. She was one of the political giants of our time without ever losing the warmth and informality for which she is justly celebrated.

PECK, M. SCOTT, M.D. *The Road Less Traveled* (Touchstone, 1978). Confronting and solving problems is a painful process that most of us attempt to avoid. The very avoidance results in greater pain and in the inability to grow either mentally or spiritually. This book suggests ways in which confronting and resolving our problems—and suffering through changes—can enable us to reach a higher level of self-understanding.

PHILLIPS, MICHAEL ET. AL. *The Seven Laws of Money* (Random House, 1974). Also, *Simple Living Investments for Old Age* (Clear Glass Publishing, 1984). These books bridge the gap for me between spirituality and money. The laws consist of such ideas as, "Money will come when you are doing the right thing" and "You can't really give money away." I was introduced to Phillips' work through Roger Pritchard, consultant for Financial Alternatives,

Berkeley, California. What I learned from these exciting thinkers is that simplicity does not necessarily equate to a decrease in quality. In fact, the reverse is not only possible but likely—if consciousness is brought to the process of making and spending money.

PRATHER, HUGH. *Notes to Myself: My Struggle to Become a Person* (Real People Press, 1970). For those who have given up on men, this man's work is a balm to the spirit. Here's one example of many, drawn from his numerous works:
   If I had only . . . forgotten future greatness
   and looked at the green things and the buildings
   and reached out to those around me
   and smelled the air
   and ignored the forms and the self-styled obligations
   and heard the rain on the roof
   and put my arms around my wife
   . . . and it's not too late.

RAINER, TRISTINE. *The New Diary* (J. P. Tarcher, 1979). I have utilized many of the techniques shared in Rainer's book—a far cry from the daily calendar diary I kept as a child. These suggestions for journaling tap into the full power of your inner resources. Refreshingly, this book does not teach the "right" way to keep a diary, but rather, it opens up many creative possibilities: to visualize the future, clarify goals, focus your energies, free your intuition, explore your dreams, your past and your present.

RAY, SONDRA, *The Only Diet There Is* (Celestial Arts, 1981). This inspiring book points out that most people who are unhappy with their weight, start at the end by trying to change their physical bodies first. Ray says you cannot separate your body from your self-image. "To start at the beginning, you need to develop a complete and positive concept of yourself. You need to be at peace with yourself, to like yourself and others, and to treat yourself with love, not punishment."

RIES, AL, and JACK TROUT. *Positioning: The Battle for Your Mind* (McGraw-Hill, 1980). I am convinced that advertising and the media are the most potent influences in our culture today. By reading the advertising industry publications, you will become aware of the strategies going on behind the scenes to win our minds and our pocketbooks. *Advertising Age,* one of these important publications, was host to many articles by the authors of this book. By reading *Positioning,* you will get an overview of how Madison Avenue uses techniques to "win the war for your mind."

ROSS, RUTH, DR. *Prospering Woman* (Whatever Publishing, Inc. 1982). Also, *Prospering Naturally,* morning and evening prosperity program tape. Dr. Ross presents an entirely new way for women to view themselves and effectively take charge of the quality of life they want for themselves. Prosperity need not be at the expense of personal relationships, health and peace of mind; rather, it is every woman's birthright to live a full and abundant life. In addition to eagerly reading this book, I listened to this tape regularly during the months preceding the public reception to my work. Sometimes I think Dr. Ross' exercises work a little too well. The tape can be obtained by writing to Dr. Ruth Ross, 1001 J. Bridgeway, Sausalito, California 94965.

VANGELIS, *Chariots of Fire* (Polygram Records, 1981). I love to use music to help me create moods. Whenever I hear this inspiring music, I feel both quieted and triumphant. After many hearings, I discovered something of great interest to me. On side one, toward the end, the very upbeat music suddenly gets very strange. The sound of "100 Meters" is disjointed, somehow off. I realized that I had always accepted this portion of the music as a contributing part to the whole. Without it, the piece would truly have lost something. Is the same true in our lives? When things seem disjointed, is that a sign that they are falling apart—or merely part of the rich tapestry?

WILHELM, RICHARD, and CARY F. BAYNES. *The I Ching.* Foreword by Carl Jung (Princeton University Press, 1950). Carl Jung became interested in the oracle technique of the I Ching as a method of exploring the unconscious. The origin of the work goes back to mythical antiquity, inspiring three thousand years of Chinese cultural history. Both of the two branches of Chinese philosophy, Confucianism and Taoism, have their common roots here.

The book presents a fascinating window into other ways of thinking. When coupled with an individual's belief that, if you cast coins or sticks in certain patterns, the book is addressing you and your inquiries personally, the I Ching can be a powerful, personal teacher as well.

Congratulations!

By purchasing or receiving this book, you have qualified for membership in Superwomen's Anonymous. As a card-carrying member of this international organization, you are entitled to all rights and privileges of membership:

- Absolutely no fund-raisers.
- All meetings guaranteed cancelled.
- Classes postponed indefinitely.

Your only obligation: to post in prominent locale the organization's motto, ENOUGH IS ENOUGH—to be consulted prior to saying yes to any new obligation, assignment or commitment.

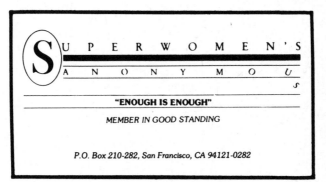

To be officially enrolled in the membership's roster, please send your name, address and a self-addressed, stamped legal-size envelope to Superwomen's Anonymous, P.O. Box 210-282, San Francisco, California 94121-0282. This way, we can ensure that you hear about any variety of offerings from Superwomen's Anonymous, guaranteed not to teach you how to cope, manage or juggle.